THE FIFTH SPARROW

THE
FIFTH SPARROW

By

RITA F. SNOWDEN

LONDON
THE EPWORTH PRESS

FIRST PUBLISHED IN 1964
© THE EPWORTH PRESS

Book Steward
FRANK H. CUMBERS

*Printed in Great Britain by Richard Clay and Company Ltd.,
Bungay, Suffolk*

In gracious memory of Dr W. E. Sangster.

'All that he came to give,
He gave and went again:
Yet have I seen him live,
And owned my friend, a king:
All that he came to give
He gave and I, who sing
His praise, bring all I have to bring.'

Contents

vii

Introduction

I WAKEN EACH morning to the busy concerted chat of sparrows in the eaves. They are cheerful little fellows. Their appearance needs no description, and their call is a penetrating *chissip*.

The sparrows of the Holy Land are not quite the same, but they share many bold, familiar habits. They love to spend their life close to human habitation. In Jerusalem I have seen nest after nest in the crevices of the city walls. In some of the less-used streets the little birds become so cheerfully noisy as to overpower every other sound.

So common were they in our Lord's day that they became the cheapest food of the poor. As a lad, He must often have accompanied Mary to the market, or when old enough, have done the family messages Himself, clutching His tiny coins. Past the well-stocked stalls of rich foods that enjoyed the patronage of the well-to-do, He would make His way to where were offered piles of the little creatures, plucked and trussed on slender wooden skewers. And He remembered those transactions all His days. When He spoke of '*two sparrows sold for a farthing*' (Mt 10²⁹) and again, '*five sparrows sold for two farthings*' (Lk 12⁶) He was not momentarily confused. For that was how things were— when He could afford the larger sum, He knew as well as any member of a poor family, *He got one thrown in for nothing*. So little were sparrows valued! 'Yet,' said He, 'one of them shall not fall on the ground without your Father.' And moving at once to His familiar 'how-much-more' argument, He added: 'Fear ye not, ye are of more value than many sparrows.'

Those who listened to Him were not slow to understand the significance of the little fifth sparrow. And this is something which in this age we need to learn anew. We move in a bewilderingly large universe, where little people in large societies are liable to be lost and men probe outer space. Attempting to tell us something of the relationship of the world in which we live, to the universe around us, a British scientist lately said: 'I want you to imagine an entirely empty London Bridge Station. I want you to imagine a speck of dust somewhere near one of the exits. That,' said he, 'is the sort of relationship which this planet on which we live, bears to the particular universe in which we live.'

No wonder the importance of the individual soul is liable to be lost—only religion has anything to say about inherent spiritual values. 'Jesus Christ,' as Harnack tellingly reminds us, 'was the first to bring *the value of every human soul* to light, and what He did, no one can ever more undo.'

The worth of the little fifth sparrow means that high or low, every one of us counts in the sight of God—even in this space-age. It's a staggering thought; but it's the Gospel!

First Things First

ALL OVER the world young nations with newly gained independence are coming blinking into the sun. But it came as a shock to read the inscription on the statue of Kwame Nkrumah, in Accra, Ghana: '*Seek ye first the political kingdom and all things will be added unto it.*'

Such a manipulation of our Lord's familiar words—if it does nothing else—jerks us back to a consideration of His meaning.

Plainly, He was no dreamy mystic, concerned exclusively with souls. His message and ministry were life-size. He lived in a human body, He hungered, He thirsted, He knew weariness, He felt the political and religious tensions of His time. He lived among people 'on the bread line'—carpenters, housewives, shepherds, fishermen. He felt for the host in an emergency, who had to knock-up a neighbour at midnight; He understood the dilemma of a craftsman with a withered hand; He knew the feeling of scraping up last coins, like the widow with two mites; He was familiar with youthful patriotism—Simon Zelotes was one of His twelve. He knew that people wanted significance, and had clamant material needs.

With all their differences, He saw that life for each reached out from some central value, wanted more than any other thing. But if a man, said He in effect, must do this, let him make sure that that on which he sets his heart is big enough for one made in the image of God. Material things he must have, in his personal life, in a community set-up, in a material world; but let him

Seek first the Kingdom of God, and His righteousness; and all these things shall be added unto him (Mt 6³³).

'Do not touch Christianity,' said Dr Henry Drummond, 'unless you are willing to seek first the Kingdom of Heaven.' But our Lord is saying here, Do not touch life's enterprise unless you are prepared to get your priorities right—for there is only one way in which it will work. Personal, family, communal satisfaction, wholeness, integration—whatever term comes first—can only be had one way. It is not a matter of things material over against things material—it's a matter of putting *first* the Kingdom of God.

And still it is so—in our modern world that embraces Ghana and other nations newly come to independence, international markets, hunger, and waste, nuclear energy, space-probes, frightening delinquency, increase in mental sickness, and break-up of family-life. Here is the single test of our affairs—not a niggardly notion that the Church has thought up—a law of life written deep down into the very nature of things.

Priorities are essential. Set up over the modern Mart in Chicago—the greatest shopping-centre man has yet made—are the words: THE BEST IN THE WORLD IS HERE. But can such a claim ever be made for *things*? Our Lord's words—manipulated in so many places, if not quite so blatantly as in Ghana—go much deeper into reality: 'Seek ye first the Kingdom of God and His righteousness; and all these things shall be added unto you.'

2

'From Dullness . . . Deliver Us'

SOME WORDS of Katherine Mansfield's have been walking up and down in my mind all morning. She longed, she said, 'to make the commonplace virtues as attractive as the ordinary vices. To present the good as the witty, the adventurous, the romantic, the gay, the alluring, and *the evil as the dull*, the solemn, the conventional, the unattractive.'

Don't you long to do that yourself, in the Church, and among Christian people? In a World Council of Churches' report from an Assembly are these words: 'The real dangers are complacency, lack of imagination, and *the dull sense of hopelessness that settles upon those of little faith.*'

People said all sorts of things about our Lord—but nobody ever said He was dull. They said He sought the company of sinners; they said He ate and drank where others ate and drank; in their frenzy, they even said He was a 'wine-bibber and gluttonous'. But in their maddest moments they never said He was dull. How could they? It was the Pharisees and other religious leaders, who by contrast, were dull, droning out their prayers, standing in the market-place, multiplying petty-fogging laws and regulations to lay a heavy weight upon the spirit. Jesus was not like that—had we no other evidence, the fact that little children were happy in His presence would be proof enough. 'Take your religion,' one has said, 'and present it to a little child. If it frightens him, and freezes the smiles on his lips, whatever sort of religion it is, it is not Christianity. It lacks the essential winsomeness of Jesus Christ.' He set a little child in the midst; He saw children at their games in the market-place. More than that, His first public engagement was a wedding-feast. Is it likely that a young couple would seek out a dull prophet to grace the occasion?

When His critics had finished calling in question His vital, joyous interest in life, there was still His teaching —they had to admit: 'Never man spake like this man.'

And the good news of God that He proclaimed, we proclaim. It is a tragedy to neglect it, and a crime to make it dull. 'If this is dull,' exclaims Dorothy Sayers passionately, 'then what, in Heaven's name, is worthy to be called exciting? The people who hanged Christ never, to do them justice, accused Him of being a bore —on the contrary, they thought Him *too dynamic to be safe.*'

And today, many feel the relevance of this judgement.

What is the matter with us? The world full of 'Christians'—the community where we live, full of 'Christians'—and we make so little impact? 'I hate being ineffective,' said Florence Allshorn, 'when it's leaders that the world is wanting. I hate, hate, hate *being ordinary and just nice, but dull.*'

God, who moved so gloriously in Jesus Christ, can do much with us yet!

3

'*A Bee in Your Halo*'

IF A LETTER came addressed 'To the saints which are at Sheffield', who would claim it? I can imagine refusals all over the city. And would the issue be any easier if it were addressed 'To the saints which are in Chicago'? Yet Paul addressed his letters, 'To the saints which are at Ephesus', 'To the saints and beloved brethren in Christ which are at Colossae', 'To all that be in Rome, beloved of God, called to be saints'. And those letters were delivered. To narrow the area, if a letter were addressed, 'To the saints which are at . . .' (your church or mine) would you or I receive it? The fact of the matter is we have blurred that shining word 'saint'. The true saint was not perfect; pause only to read over the letter Paul addressed 'To the Church which is at Corinth . . . called to be saints', and straightway you will find him taking them to task. Far from the saint setting his mind on canonization, or secretly believing himself a candidate for a stained-glass window, he actually forgot himself into sainthood. Much less was he a person of particular temperament, living apart from the tasks and tensions of life. No one would have thought of saying of him what was said of one of our day, 'He is so heavenly-minded that he is of no earthly use.' About him there was a true splendour, a challenge—'*the saint on his knees*, his mind all adoration: *the saint on his feet*, his aim all obedience'.

Known and unknown, the saints have studded the centuries:

Saints of the early dawn of Christ,
Saints of imperial Rome,
Saints of the cloistered Middle Age,
Saints of the modern home;
Saints of the soft and sunny east,
Saints of the frozen seas,
Saints of the isles that wave their palms
In the fair Antipodes;
Saints of the marts and busy streets,
Saints of the squalid lanes,
Saints of the silent solitudes,
Of the prairies and the plains.

Wherever life finds us today, the most desperate need is for saints—not perfect people, but utterly devoted; not standing silent in a niche, but walking up and down in the world with minds alert, and hands outreached to help. With some reason, three centuries ago, John Ray said of a man: 'He has a bee in his bonnet'; but E. V. Lucas, in our own day, has reminded us of a lovelier truth: *'Many a Saint has a bee in his halo.'* And thank God for that! Think of Barnardo—and like the Headmaster of Eton, you will hardly know whether to call him 'Dr Barnardo' or 'St Barnardo'. The 'bee in his halo' was the infinite worth of every little needy child. Think of Florence Nightingale—being who she was, doing what she did, holding, as Dr Fosdick puts it, 'a great idea that has made this earth ever since a more decent and human place for sick people'.

And now what about your halo? And mine? A halo without a bee is unfurnished

4

This Jig-saw Puzzle

A SMALL BOY of eight took up fret-work as a hobby in Dorset. Today—to his surprise, and certainly to the surprise of many who know him—he owns one of the biggest factories in the country for making jig-saw puzzles, educational toys, and indoor games. His name is G. J. Hayter, and he employs a hundred and twenty-five men in his Boscombe factory.

The jig-saw puzzles vary in size from simple ones employing only eight pieces, to elaborate sets with as many as two thousand. To meet a special order a while ago, a mammoth set was made with two thousand pieces.

The fascination of jig-saw puzzles holds many long after the whims of childhood have been left behind; men and women in responsible positions—doctors, engineers, councillors, clerks, and cooks—are to be found poring over the picture being slowly built up out of the pile of irregular pieces. Gradually the over-all picture becomes plain, but it takes time and patience.

To find one's vocation seems rather like a jig-saw puzzle to many. 'The actual career which one selects is in itself,' perhaps, as Monica Baldwin says, 'of only secondary importance. The thing that apparently matters to God,' she adds, 'is one's motive for embracing it. A ballet-dancer may be—and I cannot help believing often *is*—quite as pleasing to God as a nun. The important thing is that one should take responsible means to fit into *the jig-saw puzzle of life* in exactly the spot where God wants one. If one drifts, or forces oneself into a place for which one was not intended, one not only spoils that particular picture, but deflects the whole purpose and life for which one was made.'

This is to lay emphasis on the importance of God's will for each quite ordinary life—a belief centred very strongly in the New Testament. But along with it must go also the New Testament conception of the present-day purpose of God, and the fact that our failure to find it will result in missing the highest joy and satisfaction in life. Neither, of course, can be accepted in any mechanical way. God has His over-all purpose—as a player poring over his developing jig-saw puzzle—but persons are more than pieces of picture pasted on irregular cut-out paste-board or three-ply. When that is said, one can go on to add that the New Testament conception of God's will is a positive, and not a negative thing. 'My meat,' said our Lord, 'My very means of existence, is to do the will of Him that sent Me,' and again, 'I seek not mine own will, but the will of the Father.'

Someone has said, 'The secret of the capitalist today is "*My* will be done", the secret of the communist, "*Our* will be done", the secret of the Christian, "*Thy* will be done".' But is it as clear as that to most of us—in the choice of our vocation, the disposal of our spare time, the use of our money, our plans for the future? 'Give us to see Thy will,' prays one of our day, 'and lo, the night is routed and gone!' In God's over-all purpose, embracing the land, lecture-rooms, laboratories, directors' meetings, ledgers, and kitchen-sinks, there is a place where you and I can fit in, to the Glory of God—our task is to find it.

What Use is It?

THE MANAGEMENT of a Leicester hosiery factory has provided a room where its workers can pray during their lunch break. To some this will sound an odd procedure; to others a perfectly natural and practical thing.

Some people would rather be caught stealing than caught praying. They are, perhaps, the 'know-alls', like H. G. Wells. In his Autobiography he tells how on one occasion he tried it out. He was facing a first examination in book-keeping; and try as he would, he couldn't get his accounts to balance. Time was rushing on. Eventually, in a sweat, he prayed. But no good came of it—he didn't get the right answer. And there and then, he tells us, he said, 'All right, God. You won't catch me praying again.' And his boast was that he never did. Poor fool! Prayer, it must be understood from the start, is not an alternative to hard work—a means by which one can get easily what one wants, a kind of magic slot-machine.

At its highest, it is not to get things at all—but to be with Someone. As Alexis Carrel, the modern thinker, reminds us: 'When we pray, we link ourselves with the inexhaustible motive power that spins the universe.' And to add amazement to amazement, the lowliest worker in the Leicester hosiery factory can do that.

When our Lord answered the request of His disciples, and gave them the pattern Prayer, 'Our Father', He did not say, '*If* you pray . . . ,' He said, '*When* you pray . . . say "Our Father".' To pray is a perfectly natural thing—not because a worker in a Leicester hosiery factory is better or worse than any of the rest of us—*because he or she is a human being*. When a crisis occurs —a moment of indecision, an accident, a sudden illness —we pray as naturally as in falling we reach out for the nearest steadying support. But to limit prayer to such moments when at wit's end, is to leave the great practical possibilities of prayer unexplored. For it is *practical* —something happens when we pray: things change, people change, we change. That being so, it is worth sparing even some part of the lunch break; there is so much to learn about it, that to pray day in, day out, year in, year out, can bring nothing but enrichment.

One is always, of course, in the presence of God; but to realize it amidst the concerns of one's livelihood is much more. To ask forgiveness, to get rid of resentments, to strengthen one's hope, trust, confidence, courage, to bring to a Higher, Wiser, All-loving Heart, one's fears, guilt-feelings, worries, is to put one's being— body, mind, and spirit—in the way of healing and wholeness.

And that is not all; there are others about us who have equal needs, if not the same; prayer involves us in intercession—the outgoing concern of our relationships. There is also a place for praise; for confession; and for deliberate purpose in the things of the Kingdom. A good factory prayer is, '*Thank You, dear God, for endowing me with more sense than I thought I had, and other people with more co-operation than I thought they had, and for making more of Your strength available than I knew You had. Amen.*'

A Good Accompanist

K ATHLEEN FERRIER's miraculous contralto voice
came pouring into my room, in Handel's *Spring is
Coming*. That such could come through the medium
of a gramophone-recording seemed a second miracle;
but it was of a third, making the glorious experience
possible, that I found myself thinking especially—a
miracle of co-operation.

When her accompanist, Gerald Moore, was younger,
he was given a piece of advice by Sir Landon Ronald,
Principal of the Guildhall School of Music. 'Why be a
solo pianist?' he asked. 'The world is overstocked with
them. *Stick to accompanying, it is one of the most delightful
of all tasks.*'

Gerald Moore knew already something of the art:
'An accompaniment is the assistance given to a solo
part by subordinate parts either vocal or instrumental.
Thus a song or a violin solo may have a pianoforte
accompaniment to bring out and emphasize the beauty
of the primary music.'

It takes more than technical skill to accomplish this;
phrasing, accent, timing, sensitivity are all parts of this
taxing, but gladly attempted co-operation. It takes an
artist of rare spirit—without rancour or jealousy—to
give all to bring out the beauty of another's music.
Thrice happy was Kathleen Ferrier. Gerald Moore
watched well her offering of song, and interpreted
every mood with the right support.

In his memoirs with the delightful title: *Am I Too
Loud?*, he says: 'I would like to get hold of many an

average, not to say mediocre, accompanist (some of them are well known and are what is called successful) and make them write a hundred times daily the words "It is not easy".' Out of a rich experience, he leaves us in no doubt. 'How inspiring for the singer when rehearsing,' he says, 'to feel that his partner at the piano has given the song as much study as he.'

A pianist who thinks little of his task, or who, at the other extreme, wants to shine in his own right, can't be a good accompanist, any more than a careless or an egotistical chairman can set a guest-speaker on his true way. It takes so much more than technical skill, or mere words. Happy is that guest-speaker who, from the first word of his chairman, knows himself supported; a few apt words are more to him than volumes. This I have learned the world round.

None knew the secret of the good accompanist better than John the Baptist. He had his hour, with the crowds hanging on his words; but he didn't in any sense 'pound away' to his own glory; he was without any least trace of self-aggrandisement. John's one purpose was to 'emphasize the beauty of the primary music'—in his case, the Gospel of the Saviour of men (Jn 1[36]).

And is this not your role, and mine—in the Church, in the Club, in the Community? We are not called to teach, to preach, to lead the Youth Group, the Women's Fellowship, or the Men's Club, to our own glory. When we have offered our very best, our role is still that of a good accompanist: *our utmost is for the Highest!*

His Name Lives

THE PLANE circled and touched down. Below us, settling for rest at the hot day's end, was the city Paul knew, offset against blue waters of the Mediterranean. We felt like pinching ourselves—it was one of those rare moments when we needed assurance that we were not dreaming.

Four o'clock next morning found us groping along the unlighted corridor of the hotel, and down carpeted stairs, carrying our shoes. The night-porter roused himself and shouted, 'Where are you going?' Maybe he thought we were sneaking out without settling our bill. But when he heard our purpose, ah, that was different! —a proud Athenian, he was complimented that we should leave our beds to see the sun rise over the Acropolis.

One of our most exciting discoveries was *the street bearing the name of Dionysius*. Instantly we saw the outlines of that long-ago day when Paul stood on Mars Hill. Apparently it was never difficult to get an audience in Athens. Curiosity knew no bounds; but entertained by mental acrobatics, Athenians were never over-eager for conclusions. Four and a half centuries before Paul's speech, one had charged them with taking the easy part of 'spectators in plays of oratory, and listeners to the tales of others' doings'.

'Paul's spirit was stirred in him when he saw the city wholly given to idolatory. Therefore disputed he in the synagogue with the Jews, and with the devout persons, and in the market daily with them that met with him. Then certain philosophers of the Epicureans and of the Stoics encountered him. And some said, "What will this babbler say?" other some, "He seemeth to be a setter forth of strange gods"; because *he preached unto them Jesus and the Resurrection*' (Acts 17^{16-34}). Upon Mars Hill Paul stood and began his famous address: 'Ye men of Athens . . . !' How vivid it was, as we stood on that very spot; how challengingly the record of Acts leapt out to meet us. 'Babbler', we remembered, meant seed-picker—Athenian slang for a philosophic picker-up of oddments, like a bird hopping over newly-turned soil.

But soon Paul had them by the ears—fearlessly and tactfully starting where they stood on common ground, in the recognition of something divine which the religious among them sought to please, and the philosophers to comprehend. What a speech! Today the whole of it in exquisitely lettered Greek is recorded in bronze on the rocky spot where he spoke it. It sent us again to the simple summing-up of its outcome: 'When they heard of the Resurrection *some mocked . . . others said, "We will hear thee again on this matter"* . . . howbeit *certain clave unto him and believed, among the which was Dionysius.*'

Is anything easier, in Athens or anywhere else, than to argue about religion? For some it is a favourite occasion for mockery; for others it is still a matter of such little moment that it can be put off indefinitely; and happily still there are those who believe—kin to Dionysius.

Great Gifts

THE MAN with the magic bow is dead. Newspapers and wireless-stations all over the world have carried the news. It is twelve years since Fritz Kreisler the violin virtuoso was heard in public, though he continued to compose and to make music in his own home. He was eighty-six, which is counted a good age; but for those of us who loved him dearly, not long enough. He gave us so much that lifted us above commonplace traffickings to things of the spirit. He was not only a master performer possessed of a magic bow, he was a versatile composer, ranging all the way from chamber-music and operettas to folk-dances that have become classics. Who does not rejoice in his *Liebesfreud*, his *Caprice Viennois*, and his music for *Apple Blossoms*, and *Cissy*? Between the treasured opportunities to hear him in person, recordings have kept his singing notes alive the world round.

Apart from being a great musician, he was a great man; he loved music, he loved people, he loved God.

Loving people, he had the power to draw very near to them—there was nothing remote about him. Many of those who regularly attended his concerts as he journeyed from place to place, he came to regard as friends. In seats three back from the front in a hall he visited for years, used to sit an aged couple. Then one concert they were absent. At the interval, the master musician sent for the usher. 'I miss tonight, the old couple,' said he, inquiring after them, and expressing the hope that they were not kept away through illness—'I miss them greatly; they were such good listeners.'

Many such stories are extant of the relationship he built up with those who shared his joy in music. When they came forward to express their admiration of his consummate skill, he was pleased, but inclined to wave aside too-lavish praise. 'I was born with music in my system,' he would say on such occasions. 'I knew musical scores instinctively before I knew my A B C. It was a gift. I did not acquire it. So I do not even deserve thanks for the music. It is God's gift'—and including always his wife who travelled with him and so closely understood his attitude, he would add, 'we are stewards. But people do not easily understand that all things belong to God.'

Pressed to explain more, he liked to say: 'I never look upon the money I earn as my own. It is public money. It is only a fund entrusted to my care for proper disbursement. I am constantly endeavouring to reduce my needs to a minimum. I feel morally guilty in ordering a costly meal, for it deprives someone else of a slice of bread—some child, perhaps, of a bottle of milk. My beloved wife feels exactly the same way about these things as I do. Between lavish spending and what we need, stand all the homeless of the world.'

His concerts and recordings—though he never made L.P.s—brought in immense sums of money; but the man with the magic bow was above all a lover of men, women, and children—and a responsible steward of God's gifts.

Triumphant Witness

THERE WERE just two of us as, hot-footed in the burning sun out of the blue Italian sky, we pulled the bell-rope at the postern gate. From the little convent of Priscilla a sweet-faced woman answered our call. She might have been the Lady Priscilla herself. She led us into the grateful shade of a tiny waiting-room. After we had rested, and she had refreshed us with a cold drink, she went to call the gardener-handyman. As the minutes ticked by, it became obvious that this was the hour of his afternoon nap.

Assuring us of his pleasure in welcoming us, and securing his untied shoelaces, he led us through the modest courtyard, and taking up torches that awaited him on a ledge, and handing us each one, he led us down cool, wide steps. The centuries rolled back as the earth-sounds were left behind, and we found ourselves entering the Catacombs of St Priscilla—one of the most ancient Christian burial-places of Rome, and one of the largest. Less known than others visited by pilgrims from many parts of the world, we felt ourselves fortunate to be but three.

Finding a way under the road by which we had come to the postern gate, with its bell, the Catacombs extended deep down under a large garden, which had been in those early, hazardous times of the Christian Church, the private burial place of a noble Roman family to which Priscilla belonged. Out of her charity, she set aside an adjacent area to be used as there was need, by her fellow-members of the Christian community in Rome. From time to time between the second and fourth centuries, the cool galleries had been lengthened and deepened.

Every now and again we came upon wider excavations that served as small chapels—beautifully tended, and set out still as if for private worship. On ledges were simple flowers, shasta daisies, lovingly and freshly placed; it was moving to come upon them. The symbol of the fish was there again and again—mark of the earliest followers of Christ; and on the chamber walls, wrought by those same valiant witnessing people, were various biblical representations—The Madonna and the Child, the coming of the Magi, the Good Shepherd, the miracle of the Loaves and Fishes, the Crucifixion, and recurring with great significance for those whose faith set them there, reminders of His triumphant Resurrection!

It was an experience of humble recollection, unmatched for us by anything else in Rome. Much had changed with the centuries—the Forum, the Colosseum, and many a spot beside the Tiber—witnessing to the marching power and the proud cruelty of the sword, but here, undimmed, was the triumphant witness of a living faith in a Living Lord.

> *How many miles to mighty Rome*
> *That held the world in fee?*
> *How far to fare ere I may view*
> *Its marbled majesty?*
> *Oh, Rome was mighty yesteryear—*
> *Now Caesar's dead and gone,*
> *And crumbling lost magnificence*

30

Is all he looked upon.
How many miles to Calvary?
A step adown the lane—
The little chapel's table set
With bread and wine again.

Not on the Borders

WHEN I STOOD under the sky in that great ruined circle of cruelty we call the Colosseum, I knew I was on holy ground. It was a costly business to be a Christian once; there is a cross there today to prove it. It is raised appropriately enough, just in front of the ruined royal box of Caesar, and in sight of the towering seats of senators, aristocracy, vestal virgins, and the common rabble.

Luke spoke movingly of 'Paul and Barnabas, *who risked their lives* for the sake of our Lord Jesus Christ' (Acts 15²⁶, Moffatt). And Paul himself referred to Priscilla and Aquila, in the same spirit of devotion; but there were countless un-named ones who risked as much.

Discipleship, our Lord said from the very beginning, would be like that. He left no one in doubt. ' "Teacher, I will follow you anywhere," ' said one; Jesus said to him: "Foxes have holes, wild birds have nests, but the Son of man has nowhere to lay His head." ' (Mt 8²⁰, Moffatt). 'Whoever,' He added, 'wants to save his life will lose it, and whoever loses his life for my sake and the gospel's will save it' (Mk 8³⁵, Moffatt). The kind of discipleship to which I call you, said He, is like that.

And it is the glory and the amazement of the Christian story that thousands were ready. The Greek word for *witness* and the word for *martyr* were one and the same (*martus*). Christianity spread throughout the Roman Empire, not as the result of a few eloquent tongues, but as the outcome of the extraordinary risks that ordinary Christians were prepared to take. 'The infection,' said Pliny in the first century, speaking of the Faith, 'has spread through cities, villages, and country districts.' 'Fullers and weavers and teachers,' said Celsus, in the next century, 'are constantly talking about Jesus.'

But it was risky.

Disciples of Jesus are not thrown to the lions nowadays. Perhaps it might not be a bad thing if we were. So few of us bear the marks of true witnessing, much less rejoice in the risk of it. We're hoping that life will be sweeter and more significant in the little circle in which we move, if we embrace the Christian way of life—we're not looking for risk.

Young Bonhoeffer, of our day, who fell into the hands of the Nazis, for his Christian faith, and was cast into prison to await execution, wrote: 'I would like to speak of God *not on the borders of life*, but at its centre, not in weakness but in strength, not in man's suffering and death, but in his life and prosperity.'

And that is the authentic Christian note—if our religion is to be worthy of the Master we serve it must give up loitering on the borders and take the risk of coming to terms with life where it is most intensely lived.

Many Blessings

IN A LITTLE village in Denmark is a graveyard, and in that graveyard one of the most strikingly Christian inscriptions: 'Tak for Alt'—'*Thanks for everything!*'

Most of us, having given up that old mission-hymn, with its chorus:

> *Count your many blessings, name them one by one,*
> *And it will surprise you what the Lord hath done,*

ought to be on the look-out for another—a little less jingly, a little more dignified, but carrying the same meaning. For we can't get on without gratitude. Our blessings are so many, and so diverse; it is not surprising to find the dictionary making two or three jabs at a definition: 'a blessing,' it says, 'is a gift of God, or nature, a thing one is glad of.'

It was heart-warming to hear Tom Skillen—speaking over the B B C—recall his listeners to a spirit of gratitude. 'I've served as a regular soldier,' he began, 'and I've run a stall in the old Caledonian Market, but it was as a boy in my father's boot shop that I learnt my first lessons from life. It was in those good old days when money was about as plentiful as daisies in a desert.

'One afternoon a tubby little lady brought in her husband's boots for soling and heeling. Early next morning she panted back into the shop. "Started 'em?" she gasped. Dad answered, "No." "Thank goodness—only do the right one. He's been run over and might lose his left leg." She was gone and we were silent. I didn't know whether to laugh or not. At last I ventured a remark about Hard Luck. "Hard Luck!" roared my Irish father. "Only miserable people speak of Hard Luck. Mr Jones has still one leg; Mrs Jones has saved eighteen pence; and we've only lost half a customer. *Count your blessings, lad. Count your blessings.*" Since then I've tried to do just that,' added the broadcaster to whom I chanced to be lending an ear.

I have listened to much since, but to nothing more essential than that quaintly spoken word on 'thanks for everything'.

One's blessings are so constant—the experience of life, the sky over one's head, the miracle-producing earth under one's feet, love and faith and hope and courage and wonder mingling to nourish one's spirit, fellowship with one's fellows, books, music, laughter, and the daily chance to serve. And as a Christian—undergirding all—is the most gracious revelation of God, in Christ. Paul writes of it in his beautiful little letter to Philemon: 'My prayer,' he says, 'is that your fellowship with us in our common faith may deepen the understanding of *all the blessings* that union with Christ brings us' (Philemon 1⁶, *N.E.B.*).

And Sunday by Sunday still we Christian people take upon our lips 'The General Thanksgiving', to express our own thanks for all the free, undeserved good things that we know: 'We bless Thee for our creation, preservation, and *all the blessings* of this life, but above all for Thine inestimable love in the redemption of the world by our Lord Jesus Christ.'

The Chips

ONE OF my happiest hours in European travel proved as unexpected as it was unorthodox. Alighting from a tour-bus in a little clearing in the Bavarian Forest I had the privilege and satisfaction of helping a woodcutter with a sharp-edged axe. I can remember yet—and always shall—that sweet-smelling pine-wood. Stroke by stroke we added to it; and from nowhere, as it seemed, in that lonely spot, folk appeared to see a mad English-woman splitting pine-wood. But I enjoyed it. All my life I've loved an axe, since I served my apprenticeship on the family kindling. And thereafter, added strength and skill were eagerly seized on autumn by autumn as the winter's wood supply came into perspective.

Doctor Calhoun tells of a certain professor who hired a man during an experiment, to hit a log with the reverse side of his axe. Though he paid him more than the ruling wage, he only lasted out half-a-day. Said he, '*I must see the chips fly!*'

I understand that exactly; not only in wood-chopping, but in a thousand other activities. The essential need of each of us in doing a hard, slogging job is to know that we're doing something useful. And the chips are the sign of that! Once assured that we're not wasting our energies we can carry on endlessly.

I must have a review in a journal, a letter from a reader, a word from a listener when I've written an article or book, or poured out my heart in public utterance. These do not make me proud—far from it, they are more likely to make me exceedingly humble—but they do help me to see 'the chips' flying, to persuade me that I'm not wasting my life. This week I talked with a teacher in a tiny country school, half-way through her career. We fell to comment on a certain inspector known to both of us. 'Oh, I love his visits,' said my teacher-friend, 'not that his standards are any less exacting than the others; but somehow he makes one feel that even this job with a handful of children in this out-of-the-way place is worth doing.'

'Blessed are those who heal us of our self-despisings,' someone once said. I would add to that, '*Blessed are those who help us to keep the chips flying!*' It has been suggested that creative workers—writers, artists, speakers —need this most; I don't agree. It seems to me that *none of us can carry on once a sense of futility invades the daily task.* No one better understood this than Dick Sheppard. He saw it as an important part of his ministry, set down in the midst of people—but not of his only, of *yours and mine.* 'I do not think it is realized,' he said on one occasion, 'how much help and encouragement can sometimes be sent through the medium of the postman. If you look into your own memory you will probably find that the encouragement, or the comfort, that some letter once brought is amongst your most cherished possessions. A letter to someone going through rough times, or far away, or starting new work, are amongst those signs of human interest and affection which I think should come from the love of God—no one is too busy to think out acts like this.'

The Power of Print

THE CHURCH hasn't yet fully wakened to the power of print—and it must, if a great opportunity is not to be lost.

Of the power of print there is no least doubt. Two outstanding modern ministries come to the forefront of my mind—one that of a woman, one of a man. A young shop apprentice working from sixty-five to eighty hours a week, Margaret Bondfield, needed an occasional snack between meals. Wages were small, but she could afford fish-and-chips. As she was about to throw away the newspaper wrapping her gaze on one occasion was suddenly arrested by an appeal to women shop-assistants to share in the fight for better conditions. From that moment, life for Margaret Bondfield was a new thing—set out in cold print, the call to join the Shop Assistants' Union reached her with the urgency of a crusade. She not only joined, she began to equip herself to speak in public, to write, and to organize. From fish-and-chips to dinners in Downing Street may seem a far stretch, but it was all there in that page of print—her early Parliamentary career and ultimate service as the first woman to achieve Cabinet rank.

A similar element presents itself in the early career of Albert Schweitzer. Already qualified above the average thirty-year-old—an exponent of the organ music of Bach, a theologian, and a preacher at St Nicholas' Church, Strasbourg—suddenly one evening his eye caught sight of an appeal for the Congo, printed in the *Paris Evangelical Mission Magazine*. He saw in an instant what he had to do; for the next six years he gave himself to a course of medicine. That scrap of paper gave to our world Dr Albert Schweitzer.

The power of print may not always be so dramatic—but who can say that it won't be? Certainly, in this materialistic age, there is scarcely anything quite so penetrating. The Communists know that; and in the countries newly coming to responsibility they have lost no time in matching awakening literacy with reading-matter, attractive, and to hand. A unique opportunity faces the Christian Church all over the world where these people come into the inheritance of literacy. They will not lack the printed word; if Christians don't provide it, somebody else will.

Supplementing the expert training of those who serve through the pulpit at home and abroad, we must find men and women equally trained for the ministry of print. The Church that confines itself to Sunday services, week-day missionary meetings, and evening clubs, is failing in its duty. Surrounding the relatively few of us inside, are the masses outside. *If the old image of the Church is to be broken down, and a new adventure in living is to begin, we have to put our hearts into this; and we have to put our money into it*, not in the listless way many of us do at present. God will not let us off lightly, if we fail in our task of giving priority to one of the greatest media. No Christian magazine or paper must be allowed to live that isn't bridging the gaps between God and man, and man and man.

Golden Crocuses

I AM GAZING at three golden crocuses. A friend brought them fresh from her garden an hour ago. Crocuses are always a miracle in my eyes, and these seem to have a specially rich gold, as if a little of the sun's own glory was shining through them.

Wordsworth spoke of his heart leaping up when he beheld a rainbow in the sky; my heart leaps when I behold a crocus in the earth. Old Gerard, in his *Herball*, at the end of the sixteenth century, described them as 'Floures of a most perfect shining yellow colour, seeming afar off to be a hot glowing coal of fire'. I wouldn't describe crocuses that way—but then, no description that I have attempted in the last hour is any more successful.

I remember my speechlessness as I came upon the green-sward covered with them one morning beside the Cam in Cambridge. It was a crisp spring morning— I was glad of woolly gloves and scarf—but there were the crocuses! Old Hanbury, succeeding Gerard, at the end of the eighteenth century, made an attempt to describe them. 'They are all of them,' he said, 'very beautiful'—and to that I would add—'*and very courageous*'.

I understand the Rev. Sydney Smith's exclamation as he came on a crocus lifting its delicate petals above the snow, 'The Resurrection! The Resurrection!' And in our own day, Canon Sinker is as ecstatic. 'Crocuses,' he says, 'seem to greet God with the "Hallelujah Chorus"!'

Snow can intimidate us, but crocuses do not wait till everything is propitious. That is why the translators of the *Revised Standard Bible*, it seems, render a well-known passage in Isaiah: 'The wilderness and the dry land shall be glad, the desert shall rejoice and blossom; *like the crocus* it shall blossom abundantly' (Isa 35[1-2]). Knowing how reluctant we are likely to be to lose 'the rose' of the familiar *Authorized Version*, for 'the crocus', a little note is added to justify the change.

It is a new thought, and yet wholly in keeping with the outstanding courage of the crocus. '*We need more crocuses among humans*,' says Dr Halford Luccock, late Professor of Preaching at Yale Divinity School, '*people who take the first possible—or impossible—chance at getting something worth-while done. The world has moved forward on the ventures of crocus-minded people.* When the Apostle Paul sailed across the narrow sea from Asia to Europe,' the Doctor reminds us, 'there was to human view, not a chance that he would ever make a dent on Europe with the story of a condemned criminal executed in Palestine.' Yet he did—and the Gospel of the Crucified, Risen Christ came to Europe, and in time, to us. It was a courageous undertaking. 'Paul,' says the Doctor, 'was a crocus, pushing up in the dead of winter.'

And there are any number of like examples in history!

Today, the Church in the world needs crocus-minded men and women, who will not wait till everything is propitious!

The Whole Sun

I KNOW A quiet country spot not far from here, where, given a sunny day, I can be sure of finding a lizard lying in the sun. His mossy-green colouring merging with the stones, blessed by a wide bar of sunlight, brings to the front of my mind immediately Colette's words: 'The earth belongs to anyone who stops for a moment, gazes and goes on his way, *the whole sun belongs to the lizard who basks in it.*'

Of the latter statement I have no least doubt—I have paused so often in that quiet country spot—nor have I any doubt of the earlier statement: '*The earth belongs to anyone who stops for a moment, and goes on his way.*' The witness of many choice spirits confirms it.

I think of old Izaak Walton, in the gentle English countryside, fishing-rod up-raised against the sky, basket set down beside him on the bank of a small meandering stream, birds calling to their mates, children gathering wild-flowers in the woods. 'The squire on the hill,' he says, 'has a fence around this land; he thinks he owns it, and he has given me permission to fish here; but *I am the one who owns it.*' Exactly!

Nearer my own time, Richard Jefferies, driven indoors to fight a desperate battle with tuberculosis, underlines the same rich discovery. Looking back on his adventures out of doors, he says: "Every blade of grass was mine as if I had planted it. All the grasses were my pets. I loved them all. Perhaps that is why I never had a pet. Why keep pets when every wild hawk that passed over my head was *mine*? . . . Oh happy, happy days! So beautiful to watch; and *all mine!*'

And if against the witness of two men—for balance—I must set beside my own that of another woman, let it be that of Michael Fairless, the author of that choice little thing, *The Roadmender*. A confirmed invalid, shut into her room ten feet by six, she writes of the daffodil-covered island in the midst of the river on which she has spent so many happy hours: '*It is all mine* to have and to hold, without severing a single stem, or harbouring a thought of covetousness; mine as the whole earth is mine, to appropriate to myself without the burden and bane of earthly possession.' Now this is a great discovery that you and I—following the lead of the lizard, and these choice spirits—have got to make in the spiritual world. Immeasurable riches are ours; but so many of us seem to go on our way without realizing this, or appropriating them. Paul would be horrified at our poverty. To his friends in the early Church he wrote, what a modern translator has been at pains to try to make real to us (1 Cor 3^{21-3}, Moffatt): '*For all belongs to you; Paul, Apollos, Cephas, the world, life, death, the present and the future—all belongs to you; and you belong to Christ, and Christ to God.*'

God means us to be rich—and to know it!

It's Cricket . . .

CRICKET IS like Love—very difficult to explain to outsiders. Try taking an American friend to Lord's, or entertaining him on the shady fringe of your village cricket-ground. 'Naturally,' says one from across the Atlantic, 'cricket, a profound, subtle game, cannot be probed to its depths by the casual visitor. . . . Cricket is fundamental to England, like canals in Venice, or snails in Paris, or glaciers in Switzerland. . . . Americans are constantly making dreary, ignorant jokes about cricket. They say that cricket is played in slow motion.'

But Americans are not the only ones. The small boy who tried to explain the game to his French friend had the same difficulty. 'I am in my form's Eleven. It is called an Eleven because there are eleven men, which in our case are seven boys and four girls. If you haven't ever played cricket I will describe it for you. You have two teams. One team is out in the field, and that one isn't in yet. Each batsman in the team that is in goes out, and when he is out he comes in. Then another man goes in until he's out. When they're all out, they come in. One man is "not out" but he still has to come in although he's "not out", because all the men who have not been in have to go out so that they can be in so that someone can get them out.'

There are a few who can put this wonder into words —Neville Cardus, and one or two following in his train —but they are surely the gifted of high heaven; for the rest of us it is easier to watch it done, than to explain it.

And Love is like that. Casting around for words to

explain essential Christianity, Harnack hit on the happy description: '*Infinite Love in ordinary intercourse.*' Paul gave us his immortal thirteenth chapter of first Corinthians. Learned scholars and humble saints have explained the difference between the Greek words for Love—*Eros*, love of beauty, fired with passion and laden with desire; *philia*, the unselfish, steady feeling of a man for his friend; *philadelphia*, used only of actual kinship; *philanthropia*, expressive of a kindly general attitude towards mankind. And then there is the great Christian word, *Agape*. It is this—found in none of the heathen writers—baptized as it were into beauty, within the bosom of Christianity, that best shows what we are after. But more than explanations are needed. Professor Tillich tells us of Elsa Brandstrom. Her father at one time was Swedish ambassador to Russia. At the beginning of the First World War she was in St Petersburg when German prisoners-of-war were being driven through the streets on the way to Siberia. From that moment she knew that Love was something she had to do—not just talk about. She became a nurse, visiting prison-camps. After the war, her practical help among unspeakable horrors gave way to relief-work among the children of prisoners-of-war of both sides. Professor Tillich says of Elsa: '*We never had a theological conversation. It was unnecessary. She made God transparent in every moment. For God, who is Love, was abiding in her,* and she in God.'

Punch and Judy

Our OLD friends Punch and Judy are three hundred years old. The mere mention of their names recalls happy childhood experiences. Even in these sophisticated days it is estimated that there are about a hundred and fifty shows still in existence throughout Britain—some part-timers, the hobby of those who show them.

Someone has unearthed the interesting information that Samuel Pepys mounted the first show in Britain in the portico of St Paul's Church. So it is only fitting that in the same portico, beyond the fruit and vegetable market of Covent Garden, another should be mounted as part of the celebration, a service held, and a commemorative plaque unveiled. It seems plain enough that the clergy were not always so co-operative; and one doesn't blame them. There exists a letter from the under-sexton, addressed to *The Spectator*, in 1711. 'Sir,' it begins, 'I have been for twenty years under-sexton of this parish of St Paul's, Covent Garden, and have not missed tolling in to prayers six times in all those years; which office I have performed to my great satisfaction, till this fortnight last past, during which time *I find my congregation take the warning of my bell, morning and evening, to go to a puppet show* set forth by one Powell under the Piazzas. . . . I desire you will lay this before the world, that I may not be made such a fool of for the future, and that Punchinello may choose hours less canonical. As things now are, Powell has a full congregation, while we have a very thin house; if you can remedy you will very much oblige, Sir.'

There we have set out in unmistakable terms, the dilemma that is as old as time—*the choice between divine instruction and current entertainment*. Two striking verses in the book of Samuel highlight it. Set side by side, they read: 'Then Saul drew near to Samuel and said, Tell me, I pray thee, where *the seer's house is*' (1 Sam 9¹⁸), and a few chapters on: 'And Saul said unto his servants, Provide me now *a man who can play well*, and bring him to me' (1 Sam 16¹⁷).

Before we sit down to read the in-between verses, we know that something has happened—a man who set out seeking the seer's house is seen ending up satisfied with a player. ('Bid the servant pass on . . . but stand thou still a while' was the word of the seer on that former occasion, 'that I may show thee the word of God.')

But all that has changed now—the things of the soul are at a discount—all he wants is entertainment! Poor Saul! Poor under-sexton—the bell for prayers has become a call to a puppet-show!

These warnings of history—sacred and secular—have a relevancy for us in the press of life today. Divine instruction and current entertainment have each a real place in our lives—let no one doubt that—*but neither will take the place of the other*. Nor will it do just to 'jolly-up' our worship. Look at the plight of Saul; and listen to the plea of the under-sexton!

As Fresh as Ever

WITH THE air full of bird-song and my heart full of dreams, I wandered about the cathedral close of Salisbury—*New Sarum*, to mark it off from *Old Sarum* where the centre of worship once stood. Once, when a difference between soldiers and the servants of the Church reached a climax at Old Sarum, the monks returning from a procession found themselves locked out of their church. At that—according to the story—Bishop Poore ordered an arrow to be shot from Old Sarum into the watered valley below, and there they built, where Salisbury stands today.

Seven hundred years is time enough in which to fashion an account of a change of site. But there is one association with Sarum that never ages, and it is much in my mind as I recall that lovely morning in the precincts of Salisbury. Before the Reformation, the Latin services had become rather difficult for an ordinary worshipper; he was encouraged to carry to church with him a small book of devotions called a Primer. From diocese to diocese, as need arose, and from century to century, such was revised. The last put out, in 1558, was the *Sarum Primer*. Short-lived though it seems to have been—since almost at once, Mary died, and Elizabeth came to the throne—it managed to preserve for us one of the choicest expressions of the human spirit:

> *God be in my head,*
> *And in my understanding;*

> God be in my eyes,
> And in my looking;
> God be in my mouth,
> And in my speaking;
> God be in my heart,
> And in my thinking;
> God be at mine end,
> And at my departing.

Catholic and Protestant, it is a prayer common to us all—a prayer for the divine Indwelling. Overlaid through centuries, it was rediscovered by Dr Strong, Dean of Christ Church, Oxford, when editing *The Oxford Hymn-book*. Its present tune—and general appeal —we owe to Sir Walford Davies, and the London Choirs' Festival.

It covers the whole of one's being, during the whole of life.

Shortly before my visit to Salisbury, I learned of a day when Wilfred Pickles of the B B C carried his microphone into a village. Among those gathered around him was a youth. Presently, it came his turn to speak. He was a little shy, but Mr Pickles asked him his age. 'Fourteen, sir,' he replied. 'And what are you going to be?' asked the famous broadcaster. 'A minister, sir,' replied the boy, much to his surprise and pleasure. 'And what do you want to say to the people?' he was then asked. 'I'd like to sing to them,' he said. And when pressed to say what, he replied:

> God be in my head,
> And in my understanding . . .

Could he have chosen better?

19

Staring Sleep

I F YOU should be in Trysull, Staffordshire, some
Sunday, and turn into All Saints' at the hour of
worship, you might notice a neatly-clad woman in the
back pew. She is the village postwoman, Mrs Elizabeth
Granger, one of the few women vergers in the country.
Her unique position at All Saints' is that of *Sleep Rouser*
—an office created two hundred and forty years ago,
when a grant of one pound per year was made to pay
somebody to wake sleepers and remove dogs from the
church.

In those days, and earlier, sermons, of course,
were much longer than now—an hour was a modest
length. In the well-known village of Bibury, in the
Cotswolds, is a memorial to a preacher who exceeded
that length. Of him, a contemporary said: 'After he
had preached an hour by the glass'—the hour-glass on
the pulpit's edge, a common means of measuring time
then—'he would turn it, assuring the congregation that
he meant to continue *only* one hour longer.' No wonder
the Lord of the Manor, fearing sleep, got up at that
stage, and quietly retired to smoke a pipe, returning in
time for the benediction. Apparently, there was no
Sleep Rouser at Bibury. That was in 1673. A few years
later—still within the long-sermon period—Addison
wrote to *The Spectator* of his pleasure in a country Sunday, and of his old friend Sir Roger de Coverley, who
undertook the task himself. 'As Sir Roger is landlord
to the whole congregation, he keeps them in very good
order, and will suffer nobody to sleep in it besides him-

self; for, if by chance he has been surprised into a short nap at sermon, upon recovering out of it, he stands up and looks about him, and if he sees any body else nodding, either wakes them himself, or sends his servants to them.'

A good deal is said about the length of sermons these days—some say that fifteen minutes is enough, others that twenty minutes is the span of human attention. I don't know the length of those preached in All Saints', Trysull, only that Mrs Granger says that she has not yet had to exercise her prerogative and rouse from sleep a member of the congregation.

But that is not to say that nobody sleeps in All Saints'; for there is sleep *and* sleep. To relax the muscles, close the eyes, and slip into unconsciousness is one thing—embarrassing as it may be, it is not beyond the powers of a Sleep Rouser to handle. There is a sleep of the spirit, when something drastic must be done to awaken those afflicted, from drowsiness of earth-values to clear perception. There is much about this sleep in the Bible: 'Awake, thou that sleepest', 'It is high time to wake out of sleep.' Our modern sermons may seldom exceed twenty minutes in length, but the challenge remains. Addressing young ministers in training Dr Halford Luccock, Professor of Preaching at Yale Divinity School, says: 'Sleep is an enemy of preaching; most often not snoring sleep, not even nodding sleep, but just *staring sleep.*'

In Britain, Dr W. E. Sangster, one of our most beloved and sought-after preachers, was at pains to underline this danger: 'It is hard to blame people for not being vigilant,' he said. *'But that is how wickedness wins its way in this world. It counts on the sleepiness and comfort-loving character of the good—and it wins.'*

20

Uphill Work

THE WORD 'criticism', like the relationship it represents, has for most of us a harsh, cutting sound. I've just finished Phyllis Bentley's autobiography, *O Dreams, O Destinations*. Therein she says of one of her brothers: 'My brother, Norman, as I now see, was an honourable, energetic, affectionate, warm hearted, protective lad and man, devoted to his family—especially at that time to his younger brother and sister—who never indulged in a harsh action in his life. But in my childhood I did not see this. To me his protective love, his anxiety that Frank and I should take the right path (right in his view) seemed an imposition under which we laboured, a *continual unkind criticism*.'

And in maturity as in childhood, that is the experience of many of us. Criticism is so much easier to give than to receive. The trouble is we are all so full of faults, that any effort on our part to point out the faults of others has to be done with exceeding love and tact, if it is not to be resented.

Added to that is the fact that we are tempted often to feed our own self-esteem in criticism of others. When it happens that way—without humility and love—it can be a very damaging thing. Siegfried Sassoon senses it, and being a poet, puts it more tellingly than most of us have the power to do. Says he—

> When I have heard small talk about great men
> I climb to bed; light my two candles; then
> Consider what was said; and put aside

What Such a-one remarked and Someone-else
  replied . . .
How can they use such names and be not humble?

Phillips renders our Lord's words (Mt 7[1]): *'Don't criticize people, and you will not be criticized.'* This rendering gets over a difficulty that has existed in the Authorised version for a long time for some of us. In the original Greek the word *krino*, my friend the Rev. Gordon Powell reminds us, in commending Phillips' version, is 'the word from which we get "criticize". Jesus surely did not forbid us to judge another person in the sense of judging him to be noble, good, generous, loving, or virtuous in any other way. The context proves that He meant we were not to criticize others, not find fault in others.'

This is a hard lesson for people like you and me. It comes no easier to us than it did to those early Christians with whom Paul had dealings in Rome. *'After all,'* he wrote to them, *'who are you to criticize* the servant of somebody else, especially when that Somebody Else is God? It is to his own Master that he gives, or fails to give, satisfactory service' (Rom 14[4], Phillips).

There is plainly a Christian art in handling criticism —both in offering it and in receiving it. And the latter is not the easier. The spirit in which you and I receive criticism, provides almost more than anything in our human relationships the measure of our sincerity. If the criticism that comes our way is unjustified, it need hurt us no more than a light shower of rain; but if there is truth in it, then we ought to see the renewal of rain in it.

21

Splendid Failures

I AM HONOURED to name among my friends a number of splendid failures. The world will never mark their epic achievement—but does that matter? They are of the company of those valiant spirits listed in the New Testament, in Hebrews chapter eleven. One can't think of them without a lifting of the heart. They are of the company of Mallory and Irvine, men of the mountains, lost on Everest, but last seen 'going strong for the top'; they are of the company of that glorious spirit, Jean Carrel, bringing his party down safely off the Matterhorn in a blizzard, but giving his life to do it. Years later, a tourist, climbing the Matterhorn, said to his guide, 'So this is where Carrel fell?' Quick came the indignant rejoiner, 'Carrel did not fall. He died!'

So there is failure—*and* failure. A man may fail because he doesn't try—like a lazy boy at the bottom of the class; a man may fail because he is found out—and his miserable doings become headline news; a man may fail because his physical stamina is no match for his spirit—splendid failure that; a man may fail because of untoward events—like a merry-go-round man at a Fair in a wet summer; and that may be splendid failure, too.

There were many ready to count our Lord a failure. Early in the record of His ministry is the story of the Temptation—He had the power, but He did not turn stones into bread; He believed in the undergirding of God, but He did not show that He believed in it by casting Himself down from the Temple; He sought to build a kingdom that should be world-wide, but when offered it as an easy certainty, He refused it. The Devil must have felt, on all three counts, that He was a failure. But what a splendid failure!

Judas was only one of many who waited for a material conquest—the unbelieving made to bow, the enemies of his people utterly vanquished. And in all these things Jesus failed him. Is that not why he was driven to desperation?

Two honest wayfarers going home to Emmaus, after the devastating events of the Crucifixion, and burial, had a like grievance; 'we trusted' they said, to the Divine Wayfarer who drew up to company with them, 'we trusted that it had been He which should have redeemed Israel: and besides . . .' So He knew what they thought of Him—He was a failure. But what a splendid failure!

My friends know well what the world thinks of them —but they are in good company:

> Here are earth's splendid failures, come
>   From glorious foughten fields;
> Some bear the wounds of combat, some
>   Are prone upon their shields.
>
> To us that still do battle here,
>   If we in aught prevail,
> Grant God, a triumph not too dear,
>   Or strength, like theirs, to fail!

22

A Hidden Bell

MANY OF the stately homes of England are open to us now. This is both a sorrow, and a joy—a sorrow that the great properties have become so expensive to keep up; a joy, that so many of us are now able to share their great beauty and historical interests.

Albury Park, the Surrey home of Helen, Duchess of Northumberland, is one such. Set above terraces each a quarter of a mile long, blessed by a little river and banked with flowers, it is full of beauty and history.

One feature is of fascinating interest. During restoration a great bell was found hanging from the rafters of the roof. Entirely hidden, how it first got there is a mystery. It bears the date 1639, and the inscription: *'Gloria Deo in Excelsis'*—*'Glory to God on High!'*

Designed to bring Glory to God, it remained silent through centuries. There is a challenge in this.

One of the remarkable revelations of the Gospels is how often men and women, hitherto ordinary enough— fishermen, tax-collectors, women of the street—suddenly found, when they came into contact with Jesus, that they had each a 'hidden bell'. Without Him, the personal note of their lives which through all time since has brought Glory to God, would have been missing.

In his collection of character studies with the significant title, *The Men whom Jesus Made*, Dr Mackintosh Mackay speaks of Peter. Who could have guessed, knowing the uncouth fisherman, that in his personality was 'a hidden bell'? But Jesus was able to bring it to light, to the Glory of God. And Peter, from being an impulsive, blundering fellow, became an attractive personality, a leader. On the western gate of the Cathedral of Amiens, those who rejoiced in this wonderful fact carved the figure of the Young Master, and on either side, the Twelve, each with a bas-relief showing his outstanding note—and Peter's was Courage! Who could have guessed that there was a 'hidden bell' in Matthew's personality—but a tax-collector with eye and hand continually on private gain? Who could have guessed that in the personality of Mary Magdalene there was—hindered meanwhile from striking its full, unique note—a 'hidden bell'?

And this wonder is continually brought to light in biography in modern times—that is what makes it so fascinating, so challenging. I marvel as I read the story of John Newton—one-time slave-dealer—whose hymns I often sing. Lecky the historian came to call him 'one of the purest and most unselfish of saints'. Who but the Master could have uncovered his 'hidden bell'?

And is He having His triumphant way with the personalities growing up in our home, in our church, in our community?

For myself, I borrow choice words that I cannot better: *'He has the hammer that can strike my bell!'*

23

Face to Face

'I FELT A little shy about it at first. I'm glad you like it,' said my friend, when I arrived in her charming room for lunch, 'few have seen it so far.'

I don't wonder that the gifted artist in the flat above had set her heart on doing it. The outcome is a portrait of singular strength and charm—a striking likeness. My friend has not been many years in this country. The portrait, I learned, is to be exhibited a little later. Meanwhile, it hangs on the wall of her room.

I'm not sure how I'd like to live with a portrait of myself.

Maturity, of course, faces one with a challenge even more difficult—*to live with oneself*. Unavoidable though it is, few of us, I fear, have the good sense of my friend, or the wit and downright honesty of Dame Ethel Smythe. A delightful story is told of her. Many women have become famous as performers of music, but women composers are relatively rare. Dame Ethel was outstanding. On one occasion, the Art Editor of the *Radio Times* sought permission to use a photograph of her in cap and gown, conducting an orchestra with rather more vigour than grace. It was not an altogether flattering picture, but she was not one to object to its publication. 'I know the photograph well,' she replied. 'Please use it if you wish. I know it's ugly, and I know it's comic, *but it's me*!'

To face ourselves is too painful for some of us, so we pretend, or attempt to escape from ourselves in a ceaseless round of feverish activity. 'The problem of life,' as the author of *Psychology and Religious Experience* says, 'is how to have a self from which one need not get away'.

Moses, at the back of the desert, looked into his own face, and down into his own soul; Paul was unready for the heights and depths of life before he retired into the Arabian solitudes; the turning-point in the experience of the prodigal lad of whom our Lord told, is set down for all time in four words: 'He came to himself.' The Greek content of the words, commentators tell us, covers the return to consciousness of one for a time insensible, as 'he came to his senses after fainting'. The idiom appeared in many languages, before Jesus used it, but only He could give it full significance. In our day-to-day relationships, we say of another's black mood, 'he is not himself today'. In the truest sense, when the prodigal *got away from his father*, he got *away from himself*—from his inmost nature, fashioned for rich and satisfying fellowship, not for the frivolities of the far country—it was only when '*he came to himself*' that he *came back to his father where he truly belonged*.

And there is something of Moses, Paul, and the prodigal in each of us—deeper than outward appearance, the inmost need for spiritual values. To know oneself, and to live with oneself, this is the first essential —the acceptance of one's spiritual nature. This does not depend on the teaching of the Church—rather is the teaching of the Church established on this fact. One of the oddest things is the reluctance of some of us to really live. 'In the sciences,' Dr Fosdick reminds us, 'astronomy came first, after that geology, biology, sociology, until last of all came psychology. It is man's strange penchant,' he sums-up, '*to confront last what lies nearest.*'

24

A Well of Laughter

THERE WILL come a time, the Bible promises us, when there will be no more tears—but it says nothing about laughter, thanks be. How could we live without it? It is one of God's good gifts, and one of the oldest. In the Bible record of our world's earliest days, is Sarah's exclamation: '*God has made me to laugh*' (Gen 21⁶).

Life here is serious—in the family, the community, the world—and grows ever more serious. So we must have laughter; it is indispensable. God knew that, I am sure, when He gave it to us. There is a gratitude about the expression used by C. S. Lewis, our modern Christian writer, when he refers to Him as 'God who made good laughter'. It cuts right across the notion that has taken root in the heart of some, that when a man laughs, God frowns. Far from it. Old Dr Cruden, who gave the Church his *Concordance* in the eighteenth century, defined laughter as 'being merry in a sinful fashion'; but there is nothing in the Bible to confirm it.

It is true, there is laughter *and* laughter. Of the most wholesome kind, the original gift of God, essential to the spirit, as sweet as sunshine and as sound as a nut, Walter de la Mare, our modern poet, has as lovely a word as any to say: '*How rich and rare, and root-down-deep and wild and sweet it is to laugh!*' Without it, life goes awry. Faith has its laughter; truth has its laughter; goodness has its laughter. To be serious, one need not be solemn. Laughter clears the spirit of petty pride and impatience, as thunder clears the air.

Nothing so reveals what is within—generosity, shallowness, coarseness, cruelty—it all comes out in laughter. In the best, there is something God-like. '*Methinks*,' says one with a wide experience of life, '*there is in God a well of laughter very deep.*'

Old and New Testaments—being close to life—also carry references to that other kind. And there is something inverted, evil, and unbelieving about it. It made its presence felt even in the ministry of our Lord. Each of the synoptic Gospels found space to record one outstanding occasion when 'they laughed Him to scorn'. Amid the sound of the official mourners who gathered soon at news of the death of Jairus' little daughter, He made His way into the inner room where she lay. Words of life were on His lips, but 'they laughed Him to scorn'. That was laughter gone bad—stripped of all its lovely powers (Mt 9^{24}, Mk 5^{40}, Lk 8^{53}). And, unhappily, it has by no means died out of the world; those of us who worship, and witness to this same Lord of Life today, meet it often—the laughter of incredulity, of irreverence, of heartless insensibility.

If life here is to be all that God meant it to be, we cannot spare this good gift; we need to pray daily: 'God of all strength and harmony, teach us to find the deep springs of laughter, in generosity and understanding. Give us we pray Thee, the grace and courage of laughter, that seeks to heal and not to hurt; that sees the unimportance of trifles instead of magnifying them; that gives us a sense of proportion by helping us to see not ourselves, but Thyself at the centre of all things. *Amen.*'

25

All Joking Apart

THE LONGER I stood looking at what he had done, the less I knew whether to laugh or cry. Did Jacob de Wet have a nagging wife? Was he really hard up? Certainly he had an impossible task.

On 26th February 1684, poor Jacob signed a contract presented by His Majesty's Cash-keeper, to paint and deliver for £120 per annum, a hundred and ten portraits of all the Scottish Kings, 'mythical and actual'—from Fergus the First, to Charles the Second. He undertook, by the terms of the contract, to find his own paint and canvas, and to inscribe each portrait with the name of the subject, 'the names of the kings most famous in large characters, and the remanent lesser characters'. And somehow he did it.

It sounds like a cruel joke; but it was no joke to poor Jacob de Wet, toiling to turn out human nature in a job-lot. What made it worse was that there was so little to go on. Who was there to say whether Fergus the First had brown eyes or blue, whether or not Corvallus had a determined chin? The result is that three of them show exactly the same nose—perhaps Jacob ran out of ideas at that point.

It is useless now to say that he should have known better than undertake such a task. As I passed from one to another, hanging before my eyes, on the wall of Holyrood Palace, I felt more and more sure that it was a mistake from the start—whatever the motive. You just can't deal with human beings that way, though there are many still in our world who don't know it.

I would like to bundle into a tour-bus every general manager of big business, every factory foreman, city councillor, and over-worked teacher—with the hope that there would still be room for some others of us—and head the bus for Holyrood Palace. Failing that—and it would be something of a task—I would like to insist that every aspiring leader of men and women in our midst learn by heart Herbert Butterfield's Christian statement, as Professor of Modern History at the University of Cambridge: 'Each individual exists for the glory of God. *One of the most dangerous things in life is to subordinate human personality to production, to the State, even to civilization itself, to anything but the glory of God.*' One of the most desperate needs of our day, I believe, is the rediscovery of the intrinsic worth of the individual. Living in crowded cities, in large housing estates, listed at our daily place of employment in impersonal terms, 'hands', 'labour', 'personnel', it is not easy.

But it does not end there; each one of us must share this responsibility. 'Remember always,' says Eleanor Roosevelt, in her statement, '*You Learn by Living*', '*that you have not only the right to be an individual; you have an obligation to be one.* You cannot make any useful contribution in life unless you do this. It is a brave thing to have courage to be an individual; it is also, perhaps, a lonely thing. But it is better than not being an individual, *which is to be nobody at all.*'

A laughing, crying appraisal of Jacob de Wet's effort is proof enough.

26

Tongue-tied

IT IS TERRIBLE to be tongue-tied—especially in times of sorrow. Who among us has not found that? Somehow then our deepest feelings defy expression. Not to be forgotten is the utterance of the old man on the fringe of sorrow, to whom Pearl Buck introduces us: '*If a man had words, there are things to be said.*' We know there are—strong, comforting, Christian things—in our sorrow, and in the sorrow of others. But when grief strikes, and we long to speak, how many of us have words?

The *first* thing that should concern us, I feel, is not our ability to speak, but *our ability to listen*. People in sorrow need to talk, even through tears to repeat the same thing a dozen times. The New Testament with its wonderful insight, as well as modern psychiatry, confirms this important point. You remember Cleopas and his sorrowful friend, walking from Jerusalem to Emmaus—it was after a burial, and they were going home, as we all have to do some time. Re-read that ageless chapter (Lk 24¹³⁻³⁵) and note how our Lord encouraged them to talk out their sorrows, before He ventured a word. This has just come home to me.

Another point is that He never belittled what had happened; to any one in sorrow—as were those two on the Emmaus Road—it is a deep, world-filling thing at the moment.

Notice also that the name of the loved Person was brought into the talk—living memories of Him, as well as the nature of His death. Some of us have to learn to do this—as naturally as possible—when we are out-reaching to the sorrowful; to avoid mention of the name of the deceased, more than most things, inhibits speech and makes for general awkwardness.

Comfort is a strong thing, closely linked at such times with knowledge and a realistic acceptance of it—a reassuring experience, not a wordy argument. The deep things that we have long known, that for the moment have become clouded, are the things that spell strength to us in sorrow. When the two on the Emmaus Road had talked out their hearts, our Lord patiently point by point drew their attention to new meanings in things they already knew.

One of the hardest parts of sorrow is isolation—the sense of aloneness—since sensitive friends often fear to intrude. At first there are many coming and going— then the house seems empty. This is the time to share a meal—as our Lord kindly consented to do in the home at Emmaus—and to find a place in the strange period of adjustment for modern expressions of the same caring.

When the two stricken hearts of Emmaus set out— without thought of themselves and the long seven miles return walk involved—to share their new experience of life in the place of death, their own sorrow knew healing. Some deliberate act of out-reach to others in a positive way, is an essential. And each of us today, believing in the same Risen Lord, must come to the place where we burst from our sorrow, the richer for it, in witness and sharing in the affairs of on-going life.

27

A Great God

LIFE HURLS us along at such a rate that it is the rarest thing to happen upon a friend who keeps a diary. That's a pity. The diarist's advantage is that he can be perfectly honest—he need please nobody but himself, his words are private. The outcome is often a record of rare vitality, an unfakable proof of character.

I've been pondering a page of Florence Nightingale's diary, one entry in particular: '*I must remember that God is not my private secretary.*' And diary or no diary, what truth stands more in urgent need of discovery today?

Preachers and pew-holders in many places where travels have allowed me to worship, appear to think God exists solely to serve their ends—a useful appendage to the American way of life, a kind of 'Senior Director' of Democracy, in the closer communal sense, a vast Will which can be manipulated, in private life a kindly purveyor of peace, poise, and power to perturbed people.

But it is a pathetically emasculated conception, that— 'the peace of mind cult' offer to neurotics in place of sleeping-pills and barbiturates. God, the Almighty One desires our worship, our love, our service, but He will not demean Himself to be 'a celestial valet', or what Florence Nightingale calls 'my private secretary'. He does not exist that in situations that confound us, we can *use Him*.

Once we realize this in the deepest possible way, an immediate difference is apparent in our prayers. About

them there can no longer be any of the blatant begging
that Jules Romains writes about:

'O God in heaven, vouchsafe to heal my leg—
To fill my shop with customers,
Help me to find out if my servant John
Is robbing me!' 'O God,' prays another, 'cure my sore eyes!
Save me, O God, from being drunk so often!'
'Lord, let my son pass his examination,' prays another,
And another, 'Help me to make her fall in love with me . . .'

Prayer is not *using* God to advance our little plans, or
satisfy our whims. This is to reduce the high act of
prayer to a low form of selfishness. Prayer is vastly
more than a way of getting what we want—it is part of
God's way of our becoming what He wants.

God is not at our beck and call—nor is His world.
Clutton-Brock sets this down strikingly: 'God did not
make the sun to be our candle; He did not make dogs
to be our pets, or midges so that we might learn not to
blaspheme when they bite us; He made all things that
they might more and more attain to that life which is
Himself.' Too often we have seen ourselves as the centre
of the universe—with all God's creation serving us. The
greater truth in this age of the Atom and Space probes,
as in the beginning of Time, is that God revealed in
Jesus Christ is the centre of this universe. His care is
ever for us, His love ever towards us—but we cannot,
as Florence Nightingale says, bend Him to our puny
purposes. '*A great God is the Eternal . . . the depths of earth
lie in His hand . . . He made the sea, He made the land . . .
Come, let us worship and bow down!*' (Ps 95$^{3-6}$, Moffatt).

28

Beware of Brik-bats

MY SYMPATHY for little Arthur was immediate. Perhaps there is no other way to learn. I visualized him sitting on the floor, holding his head and bawling the house down. The entry in Dr John Dee's 'Diary' for 27th June 1591 reads: *'Arthur wounded on his head by his own wanton throwing of a brik-bat upright, and not well avoyding the fall of it agayn.'*

The flinging of 'brik-bats' comes naturally to us; the thing we have all to learn is their tendency to come back on our own heads. Set down in the Gospel is the record of that day when the Scribes and Pharisees brought unto our Lord a woman taken in adultery (Jn 8³⁻¹¹). Neatly concealed beneath their moral smugness were the 'brik-bats' they meant to fling. Meanwhile, they played the authority of the Law against the judgement of Jesus. Never for a moment did it occur to them that 'brik-bats' have a way of coming back on the senders' heads. It was one thing to have legal rights to do some flinging—but this other matter could not be avoided. And Jesus left them in no doubt about it. 'Let the innocent among you throw the first stone at her,' said He, and stooped and wrote on the ground. And in that brief interval, they saw that the risk was too great.

Modern psychologists go on to say that we only throw 'brik-bats' when *we deserve to have them come back on our own heads*. Listen to Hadfield, on *Psychology and Morals*. 'In judging others,' he says, 'we trumpet abroad our secret faults. We personalize our unrecognized failings, and hate in others the very faults to which we are secretly addicted. We say their conduct is incredible, monstrous! We are annoyed by the incompetence of others only because we refuse to admit our own real incompetence. Most of our emotions are directed against ourselves. We condemn the bigotry, meanness, or cynicism in others because we are potential bigots, misers, cynics.'

But we cannot say that we have not been warned. Our Lord said unmistakably: 'Judge not, that ye be not judged, *for with what judgement ye judge, ye shall be judged*: and with what measure ye mete, it shall be measured to you again' (Mt 7$^{1-2}$). What clearer word could any of us want on 'brik-bat' throwing?

The verb 'judge' here, does not, of course, refer to the law court—which is a necessary part of our society in its present imperfect state; nor does it mean the suspension of one's personal critical faculty. Since our lives are tied closely to others, and set amidst the comings and goings of home, business, and social life, we have to make judgements and assess values. What our Lord is warning against is a harsh, unloving, censoriousness—the practice of throwing 'brik-bats'. We are altogether too human for that; we know far too little of the hidden motive lying deep below the so-easily-judged action. Yet we go on—even in Church circles—blurting out opinions of those who don't please us. 'Thou art inexcusable,' says Paul, 'whosoever thou art that judgest: for *wherein thou judgest another, thou condemnest thyself*; for thou that judgest doest the same things' (Rom 2^1).

29

Right on the Mark

AMONG THE memories of childhood are the long hours we spent with bows and arrows. We did not call the art we so enjoyed 'Toxophily'—we had no idea the dictionary held such an ugly word; nor did we know that bows and arrows went back to the very beginning of Bible days (Gen 21²⁰). Ishmael's bow and arrows must have been as simple as our own. Most early peoples appear to have been archers. In time, modest improvements were introduced—a bow of tough, springy wood, mounted sometimes with bronze, arrows of reed or light wood tipped with flint (Ps 18³⁴, *R.V.*). Early in our own history—in 1066, about the only date many manage to remember—both English and Normans employed archers.

Many skills have changed; but the art of shooting with the bow and arrows has remained steadfast. To-day there are about six hundred clubs in Britain, under the jurisdiction of the Grand National Archery Society. Many members favour a steel bow, others a composite one, made of lemon wood, glass fibre, and plastic. But the essentials remain—*everything centres on taking aim.* Ancient or modern, the old saying stands: 'A good archer is not known by his arrows, but by his aim.'

An amusing story is told of the University of St Andrews when Andrew Melville was Principal of St Mary's. Some of his junior colleagues found themselves involved in a disturbance. 'The devil,' wrote his young nephew, James Melville, in the quaint spelling of the time, 'steired upe a maist dangerus uproar and tumult of the peiple of St Androis.' A party went out from the College, it appears, to practise with bows and arrows. Among them was John Caldeleuche, one of the 'Maisters of Theologie, but skarse yet a scholar in archerie'. The unhappy fellow not only missed his target, but sent his arrow right over a clump of thatched houses, where it lodged in the neck of an honest old man who happened to be passing. No wonder there was an uproar. When a man's aim is as wide of the mark as that, it must be expected.

'The word for sin is *hamartia*', as Dr William Barclay, Scottish scholar and Bible commentator reminds us. 'And *hamartia* is a shooting word. It literally means a *miss*. A man shoots his arrow at the target; the arrow misses; that is *hamartia*. This shows us that sin is the failure to hit the target of life; sin is the failure to be what we ought to be and what we could be. This is precisely why sin is so universal.' When an archer falls short of his target, he fails; and again he fails when, like the 'Maister of Theologie' at St Andrews, he shoots over and beyond it.

Surely the aim is everything—vagueness is as bad as a divided purpose. And how vague some of us are! We need to hear again the Apostle's words (Rom 14[17-19]): 'The Reign of God is not a matter of eating and drinking, it means righteousness, peace, and joy in the Holy Spirit; he who serves Christ on these lines, is acceptable to God and esteemed by men. Peace then, and the building up of each other, *these are what you should aim at*.'

30

In Bright Jackets

WITH MONEY in my pocket, and an hour to spare between appointments, I made a quick round of my favourite shops. Last week they presented a tired, turned-over look at the end of annual sales; this morning they were bright with new stocks.

When I own to finding the jacket-makers' contribution a temptation, you must not think of me coming out of a showroom smartly clad. To tell the simple truth, I didn't get farther than my favourite bookshop. There, set out in bright jackets, were the new novels, travel-books, biographies. Their yellows, reds, greens, blues combined to catch my eye. Famous names and the familiar were there. How could I resist them— especially the biographies? And there were so many to choose from—ministers, mountaineers, poets, authors, artists, scientists. It was only when I came to reflect on that bright battalion of biographies that I realized that there were no mothers among them. How seldom there are! They get an occasional tribute—Barrie gave us the life of his mother, *Margaret Ogilvie*, and Sir John Simon, *A Portrait of My Mother*—each with a quiet charm of its own; but as biographies, how modest!

Why is it that mothers figure so seldom among the books that tempt the cash from our pockets and, carried home, enrich our days? It can't be that there is nothing to tell. It can't be that mothers' lives are lacking in colour, humour, tragedy, achievement. Whatever may have been the case in great-grandmother's and great-great-grandmother's day, is not true now.

A sort of bloodless revolution—for better or worse—has taken place in our time; so that in many cases, mother, as well as father and the young folk, goes in and out of the home daily. An electric-mixer, a re-frigerator, a TV set may be coveted possessions, but nothing surely, in this age of advertisers, can make up for a good mother. Family-life has its sacred and ex-clusive obligations, its rich fun and work, its rings round the bath, and socks thrown under the bed. On the other side of the door is school, and places of business and government, where important choices are made and burdens are carried.

Whatever the future holds, the unique ministry of a good mother will last. J. B. Priestley, posing as a prophet, says: 'We cannot get grace from gadgets. In the bakelite house of the future the dishes may not break, but the heart can.'

It is in the home that a mother's living biography is written. Roland Hayes, the distinguished singer, knew well what his mother meant when she said proudly: '*Son, you are the continuation of me.*' She never had the chance to travel, she never sang on the world's great concert platforms; but he knew what she had done.

There is still no substitute for motherhood—not even cuddling little dogs, or dashing off greedily to secure a wage-packet of one's own. This story doesn't wait to be brightly-jacketed for display on a book-sellers' shelves. It's a living story!

31

A Thousand Choices

I LUNCHED TODAY with a friend in the restaurant of a great store. Escalators have been installed since my last visit, and I ascended pleasantly, my eyes surveying the stands floor by floor. It was attended by risk, of course, as the directors intended it should be.

The average person's 'wants' a hundred years ago, statisticians tell us, were eighty-two—today, by the same reckoning, they are four hundred and eighty-four! Call it 'the rising standard of living' if you will, and give all the credit you like to technologists and display experts. Whereas a mere two hundred items were urged upon a buyer a hundred years ago, today the corresponding number is thirty-two thousand—and if one counts the various brands of the same article, the number rises to the dizzy height of three hundred and sixty-five thousand! *A thousand choices a day!*

An escalator ascent through a modern kingdom of things, contributes to this end, helped by striking advertisements, neon lights, and seductively arranged window-displays. But how often the passion goes deeper—into covetousness. No wonder Louis Mac-Neice, the modern poet, cries:

> *. . . fretful even in leisure*
> *I fidget for different values.*

It is not without significance that the greatest story we know hinges on two requests: '*Give me . . . !*' '*Make me . . . !*' (Lk 15[12, 19]).

And the first is '*Give me . . . !*' These words rise as

easily to our lips in this 'thing-centred civilization', as one has called it, as to the lips of the prodigal of whom our Lord told. 'Give me money!' we cry, 'Give me things!' This is not to suggest for a moment that either request is wrong in itself; but when money, in the mad scramble, comes to be the prior consideration in a job, something has gone awry; when things, coveted and acquired, set themselves at the centre of life, something has gone awry.

God knows we have material needs; He has created us to have them, and has made provision for them. But they are not all. The young man of whom our Lord spoke in His immortal story, made that discovery. The world must have seemed a fair enough place when he approached his father with those words, 'Give me . . .!' He had certain rights; and he got what he wanted. But it wasn't enough. The day came when the words of his request were changed to 'Make me . . .'

Until we each understand what that change means, we need not condemn the Communist for being blatantly materialistic—we also are under that charge.

Speaking of the change-over in his heart, one says: 'I got what I wanted, until I no longer wanted what I got.' Charles Morgan shares the experience of another who wanted to write a book. As a youth, he prayed, 'O God, help me to write a great book'; but with the years, his values so changed, that he amended his prayer: 'God, *make me* fit to write.' Not 'Give me . . .!', but '*Make* me . . .!' By way of explanation, he said simply: 'No one does his life work until he first becomes fit to do it.'

Life is so much more than things!

32

Heads Against the Stars

W HAT A blessing those people are who make us
bump our heads against the stars! We can't do
without them. I could mention half a dozen this
moment, to whom I am indebted.

Lowell never forgot the effect Emerson had on a
young audience, of which he was part. 'We went out,'
said he, 'not knowing just exactly what he had said,
but with *our heads bumping the stars*!' He was speaking
poetically, of course, but something had happened.
And is there anything to make up for it? You can have
your stodgy, literal, down-to-earth fellows, like cows
with heads down, working their way stolidly to the next
idea. Doubtless, they have their part to play, but they
are no match for the moment Lowell knew, and you
and I have known.

Those young fishermen beside the Lake of Galilee
long ago must have experienced it superbly. One has
tried to catch its wonder in words:

> *Earth joy grew dim,*
> *My soul went after Him,*
> *I rose and followed—*
> *That was all.*
> *Who wouldn't follow*
> *If they heard Him call?*

They knew the toil it took to catch fish; they knew
the vagaries of the market, and the gossip that went on
there. They were not easily taken in—but something
happened to them in that commonplace setting that,

shared with others, set them bumping their heads on the stars. Suddenly, an altogether *new dimension was added to life*—it wasn't a little thing any more, it was a tremendously great thing.

And it still is! It is not alone the preaching of Jesus, the new Master, it is *His person*. Some of life's old questions still lack slick answers, but Jesus has answers to give us about Love, and Work, and God that are altogether different from those of anyone else. Even as Peter and John knew Him, His presence changed everything—and themselves most of all, till onlookers not knowing that men were meant to bump their heads on the stars, could only say with amazement: 'These men have been with Jesus!' (Acts 4[13]). But today His presence knows no earthly limitations; this is the secret of the dimension of many lives about us.

There was nothing naturally spectacular about Dr James Denny; any student who sat under him in Glasgow would have told us as plainly as Gammie has set it down. But there was something about him; and the wonderful thing was that he was a man through whom our Lord could communicate it to others. 'It was by his handling of the mysteries of the Faith,' says Gammie, 'that he sent his hearers forth with uplifted head, taking to their souls the things that are for ever sure though the heavens should fall.'

33

Books in Bottles

I MUST COUNT myself blessed that I can sleep anywhere—even in New York. My two visits to that
great city with its head in the clouds have been so
crowded, that by bed-time sleep has been no problem.
Some, it seems, are not so fortunate. I have just been
hearing of a fellow-traveller who, at two o'clock, in
desperation, went down into the street and bought
himself a book. There are bookshops in New York,
he assures me, regularly open till three in the morning.
But I have never had need to read all night. With a
twinkle I felt tempted to ask him if those books are sold
in bottles; it seems they might as easily be had from the
chemists.

A long time ago Richard de Bury gave thanks that
'God had provided mortals with the remedy of books'.
In our own day of rush and scramble, Holbrook Jackson
speaks of books 'pharmaceutically disposed'.

To lie awake hour after hour in a great city is no
joke; and it can happen anywhere. Writing from London, Dr Joad was moved to say: 'Some there are who
read books as they drink beer or chew gum, taking them
as an opiate to take them out of themselves.'

It is something that books can do this. I can't see
bookshops in New York or anywhere else staying open
half the night unless there are many who, lying sleepless,
find life insupportable.

Richard Le Gallienne, aware of the nervous strain
of modern life, sees the time when bookshops will 'take
the place of a dispensary, and instead of giving us

prescriptions of nauseous drugs the physician will write down the titles of delightful books—books tonic or narcotic, stimulating or sedative, as our need may be'.

It is true, books have a wide ministry as we hurry through this human scene. Fortunately, one can turn to them when life is happy and good, as well as when one is hard-pressed. They have so much more to give than merely a means of escape, a drug-like comfort, or company in the night watches.

Some of us read our bibles like this—they may as readily be served to us in bottles; we only turn to them in moments of emergency, and then only for odd verses known to minister comfort, or to restore a sense of well-being. This is to misappropriate great good.

A few years ago Anthony Deane wrote a book, *How to Enjoy the Bible*. A great many people had never thought of *enjoying* the Bible. And some have never thought of it, to this moment; they read the few pre-scribed verses each night—much as they take a sleeping-draught—and turn thankfully to a novel.

Of course, it is not possible to *enjoy* the Bible unless one remembers that it is less a book than a library—the whole essence of life, set down in biography, history, poetry, drama, song, hymn, prayer, love-story, parable, letter. Nowhere is there a more glorious range, its contributors as diverse in their times and experience as Chaucer, Shakespeare, Franklin, Trevelyan, Alan Paton, Betjemann. Its background, needless to say, is not that of twentieth-century science—why should it be? Despite this, it maintains an amazing unity, never once faltering in its witness to God the Father Almighty, and to lasting values.

34

Perfect Circle

WHEN RAPHAEL called upon a friend and found him out, he never bothered with a card—as most of us do—bearing his name and address. He took a piece of paper and drew a circle; his friends knew that only Raphael could draw a perfect circle free-hand.

That was a discovery that the friends of Jesus made— He possessed the power to draw a perfect circle—and one of His closest friends tells us of it. 'Jesus, knowing that . . . He was come from God, and went to God,' says John, washes His friends' feet.

There it is: '*From God . . . to God.*' It is no casual skill of a moment on the doorstep of a friend, but a skill of all the years, culminating unforgettably!

All that follows in John's record of the Upper Room takes its significance from this. No wonder it grips the imagination when one sees it clearly for the first time— the perfect circle, from God to God! The servant's basin, the self-seeking friends, the washing of the dusty feet are suddenly set in their true perspective. The washing is common enough—a servant's task; but this night, as the little company come in at journey's end, it is not so. Those who might serve, sit stubbornly holding on to their pride—a mood left over from a dispute on the way; who shall be greatest?

Only John—if not at once, at least later—sees this question set where it properly belongs. Greatness he sees, is not in an act, but in an attitude of life. Jesus shows His perfect circle. And nothing, it is suddenly clear, can demean His spirit. All things—even the most secular tasks of the commonplace—are seen in their proper place.

If life is to be good for us, this must also be clear. We must see ourselves—because we are men and women—coming from God, and going to God. How far removed this is from the mean conception of our nature and worth that many have.

George Santayana, the modern writer, offers us nothing more than that each is 'a little luminous meteor in an infinite abyss of nothingness'. Far from a God-designed circle, his poor estimate hasn't the power to raise one to the level of the beasts. Bertrand Russell, in his turn, wails that 'man is the product of causes which have no prevision of the end they are achieving; that his origin, his growth, his hopes and fears, his love and belief are but the outcome of an accidental collocation of atoms'. With this idea of themselves, no wonder men and women find the servants' tasks unbearable! Clement of Alexandria, in the second century, describing the clear effect of divine values, says: 'Holding festival . . . God is altogether on every side present. We cultivate our fields, praising; we sail the sea, hymning; in all the rest of our conversation we conduct ourselves according to rule!'

Such vitality comes not alone out of natural good spirits, but out of a true view of our nature.

In this age of unguessed wonders, we also must learn who we are, and what we are here for—or be driven to pettiness, despair, drugs, drink, speed.

35

Fresh and Full-flavoured

IN THE German city of Luneberg they have a custom that I wish we could copy. To each couple married they give a little canvas bag with a few ounces of salt. Gifts are also given to visitors. In all, last year, sixteen hundredweight was given away in this fashion.

Now this might be counted a good way to call attention to the city's salt deposits, workable for a thousand years; but on second thoughts, it has a significance reaching back even farther.

We speak of 'common salt'; but it was not always so. There was a time when salt was so precious that it was offered to the gods; and men waged wars for the possession of salt-springs. Soldiers were on occasion paid in salt, and were well pleased with the arrangement— hence our word *salary*, from *salarium*, soldier's salt-money. And there are still places, travellers tell us, where people will barter anything in their possession for salt. *It makes such a difference.*

There was a Jewish by-law that required every sacrifice in the Temple to be salted with salt. Apart from that, in a climate like that of Palestine, salt was essential to the preservation of food. So that when our Lord turned to His listeners who lived on the lake-shore, particularly His fishermen disciples, they knew what He meant when He said: '*Ye are the salt of the earth*' (Mt 5[13]). If life was to be *preserved*, or indeed *saved from insipidity*, then salt was needed.

It was to emphasize this ministry of wholesomeness, no doubt, that the Latin Church in early times added a simple rite to the sacrament of baptism. Not only was water sprinkled on the head, but a crystal of salt was placed in the candidate's mouth, that he should not forget the fresh flavour that his new faith was to add to life.

Our Lord did not overlook the proviso that salt needed setting to tasks of this sort—to save it was to lose it. Thomson, in *The Land and the Book*, tells of a merchant in Sidon who bought a quantity of salt from the marshes of Cyprus, and hid it in buildings on a remote mountain. His idea was to avoid taxation; but the floors were of earth, and he soon lost his salt. It became useless for its two splendid purposes, and had to be thrown out on to the hard road, to be trodden under foot.

For the Christian, remembering our Lord's words, salt still carries a challenge. And this brings us to the little canvas bags of salt given to Luneberg's newly-weds. Theirs is another human relationship that cannot be all that it might be if salt is missing. Our Lord's words, translated for us into common speech, are suddenly seen in a city like Luneberg to carry a striking and urgent relevance: '*Let there be salt between you*' (Mk 9^{50}, Moffatt).

If our city fathers could see the importance of this truth as clearly, they might start giving out little bags of salt. I can't think of a better way of reminding us that our shared life and love and thought can't be fresh and full-flavoured unless something is continually added.

36

One Bad Egg

A FRIEND OF Oliver La Farge's had a Chinese cook. He sent him to a certain house to watch a cake being made, that he might make one himself. The ingredients were assembled and the mixture duly made. It was a cake which called for six eggs—broken one by one into the mixing-bowl. But as the fourth egg was bad, it had to be thrown away. Later, when the visiting cook had learned to turn out the cake to perfection, he was asked to share the recipe with a friend. He began: 'You take seven eggs; you put three into the batter, *throw one away*, and put in three more.' Delightful!

But such literalism is not amusing when we meet it in religion. The other day I passed a man in the street, with long hair and a bundle of religious books under his arm. I suppose he thought of himself as some kind of John the Baptist crying in the wilderness! Certainly he was wearing sandals—but such literalism always breaks down somewhere; his trousers and his shabby raincoat looked a bit out of place.

It is just as disastrous to read the Bible literally— every dotted i, and crossed t, carrying exactly the weight and meaning we give them in common speech today. Words change. More than that, as Dr William Barclay reminds us, 'A great deal of the Old Testament is poetry, and poetry is destroyed when it is taken *literally*.'

The Bible is full of word-pictures: 'The Lord God planted a garden . . .' 'They heard God walking in the garden . . .' (later) 'And the Lord came down to see the city . . .' (again) 'He that sitteth in the heavens shall laugh . . .' (Then in a moment of comfort) 'He shall cover thee with His feathers, and under His wings shalt thou trust.'

The same poetic language, of course, is found in the hymn-book, where we sing:

> Cover my defenceless head
> With the shadow of Thy wing.

We do not accept it literally, any more than Shakespeare's line on Macbeth's spiritual condition:

> O, full of scorpions is my mind, dear wife.

All through the centuries this literalism that is such a trial in religion, has kept turning up. Our Lord knew it well. The Rabbis disputed endlessly over the Law which forbade burdens on the Sabbath—a sensible law; but they made it ridiculous by their literalism. They wouldn't cook a meal because that meant carrying a cooking-pot—and that was a burden; a father might not pick up his crying child—because that was a burden; a tailor might not carry his needle stuck into his coat; a cripple, wear a wooden leg; a woman might not look into her metal mirror for fear she spied a grey hair and pulled it out—that would be reaping! And they went through the Law like that.

To say that we should not take a thing literally is not to say that we should not take it *seriously*.

37

As Fast as We Like

M Y CHEERFUL passenger aged seven had often been
out in the car with me, but this was different. We
hadn't gone half a mile from Landscape Corner when
he noticed what I had only seen that morning—that my
speedometer was out of order. Immediately I had been
seized with a concern to have it put right, but that was
not at all the reaction of my small passenger. 'Oh,
good,' he exclaimed in a great burst of joy, *now we can
go as fast as we like!*'

I laughed outright at the unexpectedness of it. But
we were neither of us infants nor insane—and only
those two groups are counted irresponsible. That a
speedometer had given up registering didn't, of course,
alter the law of the land.

I continually hear talk of 'private cars', but never of
'private motorists'—for we are all involved in a partner-
ship of travel. We none of us are free to 'go as fast as
we like', even when a piece of mechanism fails.

And in the same sense, no one of us lives a private
life—if by that is meant a life with complete freedom
to disregard the law that governs others. There is no
such life. A lot of rubbish is talked about freedom—
meaning freedom to do as one wants, rather than freedom to do as one ought. One may disregard the moral
law as a smart mood dictates—*but it only means that something precious has broken down, not that the law has ceased to be*.
Walter Lippmann sees this very clearly, and looking
at some of our novels, films, plays, TV programmes
that tend to blur the edges where human relationships

are concerned, states it courageously: 'Our civiliza-tion,' he says, 'can be maintained and restored only by remembering and rediscovering the truths, and by re-establishing the virtuous habits on which it was founded. There is no use looking into the blank future for some new and fancy revelation of what man needs in order to live. The revelation has been made. By it man con-quered the jungle about him, and the barbarian within him. The criteria of truth, justice, and righteous-ness, and the grace of love and charity are the things which made men free. Men can keep their freedom and reconquer it only by these means. These are the terms stipulated in the nature of things . . . *and only in this profound, this stern, and this tested wisdom shall we find once more the light and courage we need.'*

That is great, good sense, miles removed from stuffi-ness or prudery. Moods change, as we know, customs change; but the moral law is written into the tablets of eternity. Explain this as one will, one cannot even in the most sophisticated terms explain it away. It is one thing to 'drive fast' to 'have the experience', and hide the hurts from those to whom one has expounded this philosophy—and without doubt, there will be hurts—but it is crass stupidity to think that the 'Law' no longer obtains because the 'speedometer' has broken down.

38

Meeting Myself

WHO IS THE most absent-minded person you know? Sydney Smith delighted in Lord Dudley. 'One day,' said he, 'he met me in the street, and invited me to *meet myself*. "Dine with me today; dine with me, and I will get Sydney Smith to meet you." '

God send us each such a friend. There is nothing that most of us need more than to be invited to meet ourselves. It isn't easy in the crowded lives we live. In home and community we are being continually hustled from one appointment to the next, meeting people, serving people. There is scarcely time left in which to meet ourselves. Says one:

> *If I had time to find a place*
> *I'd sit me down full face to face*
> *With my better self that cannot show*
> *In my daily life that rushes so;*
> *It might be that I would see my soul*
> *Was stumbling still toward the goal,*
> *I might be served by the thought sublime,*
> *If I had time!*

But is it only a matter of time?

Fear of the impoverished person we might find holds some of us back. To pause a moment has its dangers. One psychologist speaks of the 'interior state of apparently normal men and women. There is so little colour or satisfaction in normal life for many, that they strive to introduce it by mad escapade and foolhardy adventure, by false romance and music that is dope, by feverish activity, as *though a full diary could make up for an empty heart.*

Central in what is called the finest short-story in the world, are four momentous words: '*He came to himself*' (Lk 15[11]). It is a story that has never dated, though in this fascinating age of gadgets we have more respectable ways of getting away from our Eternal Father, and from ourselves. We don't need to go to the swine-field and the husks that the prodigal knew—we have the car, the thriller, the portable radio and transistor ready to blare, the TV. We are not any one of us 'bad' in the way that the prodigal's story implies—we're just busy, over-busy. We like it that way; lest we meet ourselves. We pity Ralph Barton, of course; one of the most gifted feature-cartoonists on the *New Yorker*, he actually took his life. In a letter he set down his situation: 'I have had few real difficulties. I have had, on the contrary, an exceptionally glamorous life, as life goes, and I have had more than my share of affection and appreciation . . . But I have run from wife to wife, from house to house, and from country to country, in a ridiculous effort to *escape from myself.*'

Tragic! No, we're not like that. But the fact which *Psychology and Religious Experience* states so realistically remains a fact: 'The problem of life is how to have a self from which one need not get away.'

39

Security

W E A L L talk about security—social security, national security, collective security. We want security against sickness, against unemployment, against old age, against war.

Many of the old securities on which our fathers, mothers, grandfathers, and grandmothers placed reliance have suddenly been seen to dissolve in the pressure of new ideas, and the frightening power of nuclear energy. Wealth, social status, education, pride of family seemed important then—perhaps too important. 'Even though I have lost,' wrote Amelia Earhart, the young pioneer airwoman, in a letter to her mother read after she had disappeared into the great spaces, 'the adventure was worth while. *Our family tends to be too secure.*'

The sort of security that ties one continually to home, clipping the wings of adventure, steadying the pace of enterprise, must always be a doubtful thing. It is fortunate for us all—as M. H. Holcroft reminds us—that in a very real sense 'man has never been secure. In other centuries they have had nothing to fear from atom bombs; but war has always been barbarous, and people lived briefly when disease swept unchecked across the earth. This does not mean that the believing man should sit with folded hands in the face of calamity. It has often been shown that the most active worker for the good life is the man or woman whose strength is spiritual.'

But implanted deep within each of us is a three-fold

need for security. *We need, each of us, to count as an individual; to feel that others are interested in us and recognize our contribution to life; and in some way, to feel ourselves part of a team.* When these elementary needs are unsatisfied, frustration sets in, and life falls apart.

It is plain that any real security that we can know, must be personal—something that is not at the mercy of things that happen around us; and that at heart, it must be based on spiritual values.

The word 'security' does not appear in the Authorized version of the Bible—and with good reason, if it is thought of in the old sense. In the translation of the New Testament, Moffat introduces twice over—as if to make sure that we would not miss it—Paul's word to Timothy: '*Keep the securities of your faith intact*', and again, '*Keep the great securities of your faith intact*' (1 Tim 6²⁰; 2 Tim 1¹⁴, Moffatt).

And what are they? Spiritual values that go down to the deep roots of our nature, and stand unshaken—the realization that the world and all that is in it is God's creation; that despite the 'God-denying look of things', He is still in control; that His supreme act in history was one of Love; that His purpose towards us remains one of Love; and that His presence, in the day-to-day demands of life may still be known, through Faith.

40

Do-gooders

'PARADISE SQUARE' belied its name. From grey skies a drizzle of rain fell. A drab place I thought it —a wall marking the edge of an uneven pavement. I found myself wondering could it have been much brighter in Wesley's day. He might have said, 'Paradise Square! Not much to look at; but this place has been the entrance into Paradise for countless Sheffield citizens!'

He visited the city first with his father—some five years before his experience of 'the warmed heart', and through the years, some forty times. Often it was at risk of life and limb; but there were rich rewards. On 15th July 1779 he wrote: 'I preached in Paradise Square, Sheffield, to as large a gathering as I ever saw on a week-day.'

It was on another 15th July—one hundred and seventy-two years later—amid a tidier, more law-abiding crowd, that I first clapped eyes on Paradise Square. We had gathered to set up a modest slab, with letters, and a likeness of the little preacher. It was a moment to be long remembered.

And now, here I was again. As I stood in the rain, before the inscription, a little old shambling man in a cloth cap came up and stood beside me. Observing what held my attention, he made one comment: 'Ah, John Wesley—*he done a lot of good!*'

It was a Christ-like tribute; for it was said of our Lord, 'He went about *doing good*' (Acts 10[38]). There is no need to turn to commentaries for a note on that. In

the first century, the eighteenth, or the twentieth, we
have no doubt about its meaning.

Within the clear pages of the gospels we see our
Lord moving about His own land of Palestine; and
our hearts go out to Him. All day and every day He
gives Himself without stint to strangers He might
never see again. And the record of His lovely ministry stands. In our crowded, self-important age, one
reaching out towards His secret, has written:

> *I read*
> *In a book*
> *That a man called*
> *CHRIST*
> *Went about doing good.*
> *It is very disconcerting*
> *To me*
> *That I am so easily*
> *Satisfied*
> *With just*
> *Going about.*

If nothing does us good, unless it first *makes* us good,
then we see His secret. Our Lord was always making
men and women good—in ways unexpected—and
there was never any coercion or pious pleading.

Unfortunately, William Purcell is right: 'The professional "do-gooder", the person driven by a high,
though sometimes sombre sense of religious duty, has
never been a popular figure.'

We know why.

41

He Didn't Go

GEORGE FEARON, of St Martin-in-the-Fields, tells of a small boy 'who when asked what he knew about St Paul, replied that "he was a restless man always moving from one place to another, and wherever he was he said a few words"'. Delightful! But there is a little more to be said—not only about the places where he went, but where *he didn't go*. The book of Acts records how Bithynia was shut to him, and it is an instructive point for us—for we each know something of frustration, we each have a fair Bithynia where we long to go.

The record concerning Paul and his companion Silas is simple enough: 'As they went through the cities, they delivered them the decrees for to keep, that were ordained of the apostles and elders which were at Jerusalem. . . . After they were come to Mysia, *they assayed to go into Bithynia: but the Spirit suffered them not*' (Acts 16⁴⁻⁷). How this sudden block in the plans came we are not told. It may have been by some vision, or some inner and unmistakable conviction, it may be that Paul wasn't fit to go on; for at this point the record enters upon the 'we' passage, proving that Dr Luke was unexpectedly of their company. What more likely than Paul's need of professional services, as on other occasions, as the result of his 'thorn in the flesh'? One thing is certain, Paul was momentarily frustrated; if it was ill-health which barred him from going into Bithynia, it was an experience familiar to very many of us.

Paul and his companion might have argued that they were not travelling for pleasure, or for personal monetary profit—they were ambassadors for the Kingdom of Christ. Nevertheless, they were thwarted; but they accepted it without rancour as the guidance of God. No bitterness of spirit shows through this brief record of frustration.

Bithynia stands in the experience of each of us for *something desired, something denied*. Viewed from afar, it looks 'the rich, fertile, peaceful, highly civilized province' others have described it—the very place where a great deal might be done, and things of the Kingdom established.

(Paul's frustration was only momentary—we need to remember that; with fair Bithynia denied, he went on to Troas, and following the call 'Come over and help us!' to the greater ministry of Europe. But while it lasted, the frustration was real enough.)

Amy Wilson Carmichael, the great missionary 'mother' of India, had her Bithynia. She set her heart on going to China—and viewed from beneath the blue skies of Ireland there seemed nothing more desirable. But she never got there; even though she reached the point where all her boxes were packed, and the ship soon due to sail. In all honesty, the doctor who examined her, could not give her a pass. She tried then to go to Japan—but that wasn't the happiest thing either, and in a year she had to come home. Then the day came when—like Troas—God's greater purpose was made known to her; and journeying to Dohnavur, in India, she found her life-work, gathering into an ever-enlarging home for fifty years little temple children, teaching them the Christian way of life, and through her books sharing with countless others of us the miracle of truth and compassion.

God give us patience when we come to Bithynia!

42

It Won't Fill any Pews

AS CHRISTIANS we don't intend to cheat; but when we reduce our Lord's awkward words to a piece of Eastern hyperbole, we do it all the same. 'Love your enemies,' He says, 'bless them that curse you, do good to them that hate you ... For if ye love them which love you, what reward have ye? Do not even the publicans the same? And if ye salute your brethren only, *what do ye more than others*?' (Mt 5⁴⁷).

We so easily accept Pandit Nehru's word, in this hungry world, as a piece of common sense—the sort of plan we wouldn't be embarrassed to introduce into a trade discussion, or a market conference. But it isn't Christian. 'If some countries,' says he, 'which are fortunate enough, think that they can live their lives apart, whatever happens to the rest of the world, it is obvious that they are under a misapprehension.' So far so good. This is the background against which we pray the Lord's Prayer, with its family petition: 'Give us this day our daily bread.' More and more we acknowledge—through the elimination of distance, rapid transport, and the sharing of news by wireless, newspapers, and TV—we have become one world.

But it is when Pandit Nehru goes on to bring out into the open the motive behind much of our sharing, that we stand condemned. 'It is not a question of the prosperous, merely out of the generosity of their hearts, helping those that are not prosperous—though generosity is a good thing—it is,' he says, 'a question of an *enlightened self-interest*, realizing that if some parts do not progress, they have an adverse effect on the whole. Therefore, it becomes inevitable to consider these problems in a global way.'

That is political talk; but Jesus our Lord and Master, was no politician. He did not talk about 'enlightened self-interest'; His word that we have dodged often, personally and nationally, is *'What do ye more than others?'* We needn't confuse the issue by passing judgement on Mr Nehru; that isn't our business—the word of our Lord is plain.

It is no less refreshing that some of our Church leaders, acting on our behalf, have the courage to take Him seriously. Following on the devastation and need caused by the recent Persian earthquake, the World Council of Churches has just announced that it will rebuild a five-hundred-family Muslim village, for which £148,000 has already been promised throughout the world.

It won't fill any pews. And lots of people who criticize our local church, when we pass 'some tin-pot resolution' about the bowling-club opening its greens for play during our hour of worship, won't even hear about it. But the World Council of Churches is doing it just the same. And each of the five hundred houses will have cooking utensils. In addition, a village school, public baths, and a laundry will be provided for the people, and they will be presented with livestock, seeds, and implements.

Well! Nobody is talking of 'enlightened self-interest' this time. We're just being led to take our Lord seriously; Christian love is going into action as Christian love. Nobody is asking, 'What do we get out of it?'

43

Things Look Different . . .

THE VELVETY dark was all about them as young
Steven Wilding and his mother and sisters returned
to 'The House on the Hill'. Though they knew the
road well, there was no chance of seeing the grass verge,
much less the deep dyke on each side. As Steven said,
with a wisdom beyond his eleven years, '*Things look
different when it's too dark to see*'.

Lacking light, men and women have trudged with
dread, often with disaster.

More desperate has been the darkness that from time
to time has surrounded their spirits. Micah, with Amos,
Hosea, and Isaiah, made up the quartette who pro-
duced the golden age of prophecy in the latter half of
the eighth century, B.C. The people's foreign relationships, together with their internal life, made up, Micah
knew, a very dark situation indeed. Assyria, that ruth-
less power, had already embarked on menacing
activity—Syria had been over-run and many of her
people carried into captivity. Israel was soon to know
a like fate; Judah, meanwhile, had become little more
than a buffer State between Assyria and the realization
of her dreams in Egypt. 'Things look different,' Micah
might have said, 'when it's too dark to see.'

But that was not all; and his people lifted up their
heads at his voice: '*When I sit in darkness*,' said he, '*the
Lord will be a light to me*' (Micah 7⁸, *R.S.V.*). The new
factor was that God was there—as in the darkness at
the world's creation, saying, 'Let there be light!' It

was not His divine intention, Micah believed, that His people should stagger endlessly.

And this glimmer of faith lived on in the hearts of men and women during the long four hundred years when no prophetic voice was heard. At last came the revealing light of Bethlehem. Never again could the dark be quite so dark! To those who had waited long, was God's wondrous light given in His own Son. No name by which He later called Himself can have been to those who welcomed Him, amidst their problems, more precious than that designation: '*I am the Light of the world!*'

Political intrigue, personal betrayal, religious intolerance, human cruelty, and all things that combine to bring darkness, were not, of course, miraculously dissolved. At the Crucifixion, the darkest experience of the spirit of man—before God's three days were fully run—the world was very dark indeed.

And then came Easter—'*when it was yet dark*'—as John puts it, every single word of his statement charged with wonder. Mary coming early to the Tomb, found the stone rolled away, and Christ risen! (Jn 20¹)

Never now—never—can the dark be quite so dark. Death, and all that made up the Crucifixion, are still factors in life, expressing themselves devilishly through the debasement of science—but Christ is risen! And because He lives, we too, shall live! That is the most wondrous gleam of light in our dark world.

44

Shut-ins

WHEN I HEAR from a friend that he or she is off to
London, there is one thing I always say: 'Leave
the ship at Southampton; it's a much better way in
than by Tilbury.' Between Southampton and the City
for the newcomer lies the green countryside—hedges,
trees, winding streams, town and village houses, green
meadows, and gracious spaces; whereas the route from
Tilbury by train brings one through Dockland's
crowded shabbiness—rows and rows of roof-tops, back-
yards, front doorsteps almost identical, and an endlessly
depressing blight of chimney-pots.

A first impression is not easily erased. I can quite
understand the Spanish girl who exclaimed as she
looked out of the train on to the pack of houses, factories,
chimneys, '*These people have no view!*' With that, she
burst into tears, adding '*To have no view, how sad a lot!*'

The most unhappy 'shut-ins', of course, are by no
means those between Tilbury and the City, though I
take pains to have first impressions spared those
cramped streets. They are not even those invalids who,
for physical reasons, cannot get beyond their own
rooms; though we do a good deal for such these days.
The 'shut-ins' most to be pitied are those like poor
egotistical Edith, bounded on the north, south, east,
and west by Edith. Locality has next to nothing to do
with their state, nor architecture, nor deformed limbs
and painful joints. They are 'shut-ins' of the spirit—
and they need more than a wheel-chair or callipers.
They need what the Christian Church can bring to the

situation. When Bishop Quayle of the American Methodist Church was travelling with a number of men, he was mistaken for a business man. After discussing the kind of goods they sold, they asked the Bishop, 'What goods do you sell?' He replied '*I sell horizons!*' And that was a splendid Christian answer.

From the beginning, the Christian Gospel has recognized the simple fact that as human spirits in physical bodies we might easily be shut in. To those who first heard our Lord's challenge to follow, He made it quite clear that they were called to an ever-enlarging experience—they were to ask their questions and go on thinking, in prayer to reach up to God and out to their fellows, in their witness to begin in Jerusalem, the place where they were, and go on to Judea, the next place, and on to Samaria, and out to the uttermost parts of the earth (Acts 1⁸). A 'shut-in' religion might be some sort of religion, but in any limiting, stuffy sense, in any self-pitying egotistical sense it could not be the religion of Jesus Christ. There was always something so whole, vigorous, and out-reaching about Him. And this must be the same for those of us who follow Him:

> *A new horizon every week;*
> *New hills, new sky;*
> *A new horizon every week*
> *To greet the eye.*

Nor does it end here; Paul caught up that confidence: 'Eye hath not seen,' said he, 'nor ear heard, neither have entered into the heart of man, the things which God hath prepared for them that love Him' (1 Cor 2⁹).

45

Two Inches Taller

SOME OF US would like to be a little taller; but for all our anxious thought, we can't add to our stature (Mt 6²⁷).

But there is a glorious sense in which what we cannot do for ourselves, another can do for us. A friend of Lord Grey of Fallodon, lover of God, men, and all living things that he found so beautiful, once explained why he paid him a visit: 'I was feeling depressed this morning, and I wanted to be made to *feel two inches taller.*'

It wasn't, as he well knew, a matter of stature at all, but of spirit.

In outstanding measure, that was a power that Jesus had. To turn over the pages of the gospels, is to see being met again and again that very human need that Grey's friend knew, and that we all know. One sees little Zacchaeus up the tree; chief of tax-gatherers, and rich, he is short of stature; but it isn't only his height that is responsible for his crouching there in the shade, hoping to catch a glimpse of Jesus as He passes below. He is hated—something is awry with his spirit. His great need is to feel 'two inches taller'. But look at him an hour or two later, at the end of that day that began so ignominiously—not up the tree now, but in his home, host to Jesus. So marked is the change in him that it is one of the miracle stories of the gospels.

Or look again—this time at the woman taken in sin, dragged into the presence of our Lord. Stay to overhear the dialogue between her accusers and Jesus that goes on over her cowering head. See the issue swing unexpectedly as Jesus speaks penetrating words, and later stoops to write on the ground. And in an instant you know yourself not only looking in on one of the most dramatic and compassionate moments in history, but you are seeing a beaten human spirit rising from the dust; forgiven, standing now at the full height of her womanhood. The future she faces is better than the past.

Or look again at two going home to Emmaus, grief-stricken, shoulders slumped. A terrible weight is upon their spirits; One whom they loved, and in whom was all their hope, is dead. And there seems nothing left to do but, heads together, to trudge home. But see them again after they have met Jesus—and having listened to His words, have invited Him into their home to break bread. See them recognize Him in that very act, alive, triumphant over Death—and see them with heads high, and a new eager light in their eyes, race back over the way they have come, to tell His disciples, 'He is risen!' They are inches taller!

And so it goes on.

Today, as we all know, there are still limits to what anxious thought can do—we cannot add to our stature, but by His grace communicated through His servants we can stand taller in our spirits. One of the loveliest things said of Alice Freeman Palmer, beloved Principal of Wellesley College, was by one of her students: 'When I saw her, I felt as if I could do things that I never dreamed of before. Even now, whenever I think of her, I have *a sense of dignity in my life. I don't know what it is. It seems as if her appreciation of the worth of things put a spirit into me* . . . I shouldn't care to go on in a world where she hadn't been.'

46

The Earthward Side

STORM JAMESON introduces us to a mother and daughter bound by strong ties of affection. The moment comes when the mother lies unconscious. 'We have taken so many journeys together,' says the daughter simply, 'and now you must set out on this one alone.'

It is always like that. We are human creatures; we may not stay here long. We can call Death what we will; but it is a journey that each of us must make—and alone, some early, some late.

A measure of fear is natural; we know so little about that experience. Some fear pain, some the human parting, some the prospect of judgement. The man or woman who faces Death lightly, we feel, has nothing to say to us. Our help is rather with Elizabeth Barrett Browning, and those of our day who, like her, continue to face Death with Christian realism. At the death of little Joe Story, the playmate of her little boy Pen, she was all but overcome with grief; but she entered into the shock and loss of the bereaved parents with words that carried for them a bracing comfort: '*I can't look on the earthward side of Death*,' said she, through her tears. 'When I look Deathwards, I look *over* Death, and upwards, or I can't look that way at all.'

And so do those of us who embrace the Christian Faith. We are not less moved by the experience itself—but we look over it and upwards. The earthward side of Death is no longer the most real; Christ has risen from the dead, and that makes all the difference.

The centre of our confidence is there; without that what comfort could we have?

Through Him, a new sense of victory comes flooding in upon our brief adventure here, a new power, an added dimension. Not only for the disciples in Jerusalem—prostrate with grief—but for us, the most significant consequences rest on His resurrection. It does not ignore our human questions—much less does it claim to answer them all. But it is enough. The truth is that in Joseph's garden, near a Cross, He not merely *survived* Death, He *conquered* Death. There's a world of difference—and because of that difference we now look over Death and upwards.

We believe ourselves, here and now, being led towards a Life too big for this world to contain.

> *Our wayside planet, carrying land*
> *and wave*
> *Love and life multiplied, and pain*
> *and bliss,*
> *Bears, as chief treasure, one forsaken grave.*

'Now is Christ risen from the dead, and become the first fruits of them that slept. For since by man came Death, by Man came also the Resurrection of the dead. For as in Adam all die, even so in Christ shall all be made alive' (1 Cor 15[20]).

47

A Haunted Race

Aloneness and loneliness are not the same, though some confuse them. 'Many young people today,' said Viscount Cobham, in a speech to our University, 'often seem so very lonely, not lonely in the sense of being alone, but quite the reverse—*so afraid of being alone that they must always be part of a crowd.*'

The origin of some of our odd social quirks—crouching over little tables in half-dark coffee-bars—may lie here; not less some of our more widely-deplored antisocial activities. Loneliness, psychiatrists and socialworkers claim, is one of the most pronounced maladies of our age. An only child, we know, can be lonely—inventing for his heart's ease an invisible playmate; a new boarding-school pupil can be terribly lonely—not sure where he belongs; a teen-ager beginning work—anxious to mingle, can throw judgement to the winds and make the wrong friends; and many in marriage—far from continual company banishing loneliness, can find in a conflict of standards, a loneliness only the more terrible for being so closely woven.

Rose Macaulay sweeps a wide horizon when she says: '*We are a haunted race,* fleeing from silence and great spaces, feeling safe only when surrounded by warm, comprehensible, chattering humanity like ourselves.'

The loneliness of old age today can be no less pathetic than that of youth or middle-age. In Britain, it is estimated there are at least two million folk over seventy-five—half of them living alone. That must not be interpreted to mean that all such are lonely—far from it—some delight to live alone, with their few treasured things about them, and their independence. Others are not so happily placed—circumstances have given them no choice. It is for these that the Church in a new and wonderful way, through her Homes, has come to exercise a widespread loving care, supplementing what hospitals and institutions can do.

In health and strength, before the years pile up, it is good to be some part of each day alone—on such good terms with oneself that the problem is never how to get away. This yields a richness, a maturity, a spiritual reality that nothing else can.

And this is not to overlook the discovery that in a very real sense a Christian never is alone. The words of our Lord are: '*Be assured, I am with you always*' (Mt 28²⁰, *N.E.B.*). One rejoicing in this writes:

> *I am not alone*
> *By night,*
> *Or by day,*
> *Or by circumstances:*
> *Neither in the silence,*
> *Nor in the city's roar;*
> *Nor as I lie*
> *At the door of death.*
> *Or stand on the*
> *Threshold*
> *Of a new Life:*
> *For Thou art with me.*

48

Behind the Noughts

S OME SPEAKERS and writers love nothing better, it
seems, than to batter us over the head with statistics.
They tell us that world population—due to 'population
explosion', that horrible term—stands now at two
thousand seven hundred and thirty-seven million, of
whom eight hundred and fifty million are Christians.
Over twenty-three million, they tell us, are refugees;
two out of every three can neither read nor write, and
every night two out of three lie down in hunger.

Statistics always sound to me terribly efficient, on a
first hearing; but unless I write them down, when I
come to use them I can never remember how many
noughts there are on the end. Statistics have their uses,
of course; but they have their limitations, too.

Clifford Bax says of George Russell ('A.E.' as he
came to be known): 'People were not real to A.E.
Never once did he show any interest in a man's background, in his hopes, in his troubles.' Types, age-groups,
climates of opinion, hands, personnel, digits on a
census-paper, people are all these—but they are more.
That is the lasting significance of Dr William Temple's
words: '*It is the mark of the Christian that he can read
statistics with compassion.*' It is not easy when they are
hurled at us right and left; but somehow the human
beings, and human needs behind them, must reach our
hearts as well as our heads.

'The modern world began,' Professor MacMurray
reminds us, 'with Christ's discovery of the individual.'
This is something precious, and costly to maintain. It

is much easier to count heads than to minister to hearts; but as Christians we are called to keep these two things in balance—*to read statistics with compassion.*

There came a day in the life of that lovely soul Margaret Ethel MacDonald, wife of Ramsay Mac-Donald, when she lost by death a little boy of five. It was a grievous experience. And in a letter to a friend, she wrote what her biographer has done well to preserve for us: '*These statistics* of mortality among children,' she wrote, 'have become unbearable to me. I used to be able to read them in a dull scientific sort of way, but now I seem to know the pain behind each one. It is not true that other children can make it up to you, that time heals the pain. It doesn't. . . . We women must work for a world where little children will not needlessly die.' That she did, as we know, in a most effective and compassionate way.

Statistics, clearly analysed and carefully stated, can say some things to us; but we need more—a Christian spirit that will quicken compassion. A complete realization of all that lies behind them, would, of course, crush our hearts; but it is perilously easy to be casual, to stumble over the noughts and do nothing more.

Today, perhaps, more than at any other time, we need to hear clearly words addressed to early fellow-Christians (Col 3¹², Moffatt): 'As God's own chosen, then, as consecrated and beloved, *be clothed with compassion.*'

49

Choose

HOWEVER REAL the possibility that we will mis-
manage our lives, we cannot have in this world
which God has created, goodness or gladness unless the
alternative is open to us; we cannot know the fellowship of the Father's family, without being free to choose
the far country. Love that is compelled is not love—
without choice it has no glory, no spontaneity. All the
way through the Old and New Testaments, the recurring word is 'Choose!'

And in our own day we hear it, like the single note
of a resonant bell. 'I protest,' said Huxley, facing a
group of students, 'that if some great Power would
agree to make me always think what is true, and do
what is right, on condition of being turned into a sort
of clock, and wound up every morning before I got out
of bed, *I should instantly close with the offer.*'

Ah, the responsibility is something we cannot
escape. There are many things that we may rightly do,
and some that we should not do—we are left with the
choice. God alone knows the risk He is taking when He
bestows this gift. Without it, life might be safer, but it
could never be as satisfying.

Where black stands out against white, love against
hate, it is easy—but do you find life as simple as that?
Isn't our position much more often that of Amelia
Earhart, that valiant young airwoman whose epic
flights I saw commemorated on a rough stone in
Honolulu, within sound of the sea, again on a striking
mural in Radio City, New York? Slight of body, eager

of heart and mind, she crowded much into her brief span. On each of her flights she kept a record, till the last when she was lost to our sight in the great spaces. Of her first, she wrote significantly: 'When I got about five hundred miles over the Atlantic from Halifax, I suddenly began to have trouble with my engine. It sputtered and backfired, and sounded like it was going to give up. I lowered the plane and flew close to the sea . . . I figured the distance I had already come and that which I had to go before I reached Ireland. I decided to go on . . . for *the hazards of going on were no greater than the hazards of going back.*'

And isn't that just the sort of choice that faces us most often—not between unequal distances, between bad and good, but between *good and good*? Dr Sangster said: 'As one advances in spiritual maturity the important decisions of life are less and less between good and evil, and more and more between *the higher and the lower good.*' This is surely the point of our Lord's story of the Great Feast. Many were invited; but when the time came, three were 'otherwise engaged'. One had bought a field and wanted to have a second look at it; another had acquired oxen and wanted to try them out; and the third had married a wife, and at the moment was completely taken up with his own happiness. *Not one had chosen a bad thing in itself*—joy of possession, claims of business, delights of home-making —only a lower good for a higher good. *But in his choice, each missed the Great Feast of Life.*

50

Talk of Money

ONE NIGHT, as T. E. Lawrence was out in the desert with his mixed force of Arabs, sitting around the camp-fire under the stars, one of them began lazily looking up through his field-glasses. 'And the stars— what are they?' came his question. That set them all talking of stars—thousands already revealed through men's telescopes, and myriads yet waiting discovery. Presently, one of the men said: 'When we see them all, there will be no night in heaven.' Then another broke in impatiently: 'Why are the Westerners always wanting everything? Behind our few stars we can see God, and He is not to be found beyond your millions.' Then the questioning one continued: 'Are there men on these greater worlds?' But the impatient one broke in again: 'Lads, we know our districts, and our camels, and our women . . . the rest is God's and the glory is God's', and he immediately turned the conversation to the *subject of money, until all the tongues began to buzz at once.*

Call it an anti-climax—but how easily our own thoughts turn from the *glory of God, to money!*

But isn't there a way to relate the two? The New Testament is full of talk of money. Far from regarding it as evil, our Lord was quick to see what good it might do. He saw that without it the Samaritan could not have paid for the beaten-up traveller's keep at the Inn; the Roman centurion, affluent, and therefore able to build a new synagogue for the people, won His praise; nor did He overlook the poor widow with her slender resources. He took pains—at the other extreme—to underline the irresponsibility of rich Dives; and the foolishness of the man with nothing but barns and crops.

'Money,' says Aldous Huxley, 'breeds a sort of gangrened insensitiveness.' But does that need to be so? It was Paul who wrote: 'The love of money is the root of all evil'—not the money itself (1 Tim 6^{10}). Many a good cause in the Church and in the community lags for want of it. Only a saint, such as St Francis, held in the 'holy nuptials of Lady Poverty', or a fool, can ignore money, and not even then for long—somebody has to come forward with food, footwear, clothing, and shelter that money has paid for, if he is to live.

So much hinges on our honestly-acquired bank-accounts, and our pay-envelopes at the end of each working-week—whether we regard money in terms of 'ownership' or 'stewardship'. To the modern disciple of our Lord the challenge is not, 'Your money or your life', but 'Your money *and* your life!' How we earn it, and spend it in the presence of God, is what matters. God doesn't expect us to be wholly spiritual; so long as we live in mortal bodies, we have material needs. But the good steward is responsible to God for all that he is, and all that he has—*the issue is not how much of one's money one must give to God, but how much of God's money one may keep for oneself.*

51

One in Ten

OLD DURGA AMA, aged a hundred and seven, has
died. News of her passing reached me through a
friend serving in the Punjab; and it has sent me back
to a re-reading of Luke's vivid account of the healing
of the ten lepers, and of the one who returned to give
thanks. For old Durga Ama was a leper—a thankful
one. Her hundred and seven years were all too short
for the over-spilling thankfulness of her heart. 'What a
joy it was to meet her,' said Lorraine. 'Without hands,
feet, or sight, and with hearing beginning to fail, she
was still radiant with a joy which can come only from
a Christian faith.'

During the last fifty years her home has been at
Chandag Heights, the leprosy colony in the Himalayas,
maintained by the Mission to Lepers and Methodist
Missions. Before she lost her sight she used to propel
herself about the colony in an old wheel-chair; when
the tracks became too steep for that, six thousand feet
up, she would slither out and scramble on her knees.

I wish we could have old Durga Ama's comment
on this passage I have been re-reading (Lk 17$^{12-19}$).
But in the most real way, her whole life was her
comment.

Ten lepers were cleansed, and only one returned to
give thanks, says Dr Luke, with meticulous care in
matters medical, and 'he was a Samaritan'. Our Lord's
word for him was 'this stranger'. That was not likely
to be lost on Luke; he repeatedly showed feeling for the
semi-outcast Samaritans. It would have been striking

if this one man—one in ten—had been a Jew; but he was a Samaritan. One can never tell where thankfulness will show itself—*it waits often in the most unlikely places.*

Certainly old Durga Ama lived in one of the most beautiful parts of the world—away to the north stood the eternal snows of the Himalayas, in grandeur and sublimity indescribable. But she was a leper! At first, few lived in the colony—a collection of huts on a high crest above the mountain valley—but with the years others came, and living conditions greatly improved. To many there, God gave not only new bodies, but new souls. Old Durga Ama was too late for her body to get benefit from the introduction of Chaulmoogra oil, followed by the miracle-working sulphone treatments, and physiotherapy. In time she became a 'burnt-out case', the disease no longer active. But her thankfulness never burnt out.

The New Testament is punctuated with thanks from men and women suffering indignities, persecutions, and worse. '*Thanks be to God,*' we catch the echo of their words, 'which giveth us the victory through our Lord Jesus Christ!' (1 Cor 15[57]).

52

Close Beside Us

I AM NOT puzzled now, as once, by the story of one who, sent into the world to search for the most precious thing, returned with a single tear. My dictionary offers a definition. 'A tear,' it says, 'is a drop of saline liquid, ordinarily serving to moisten and wash the eye, but falling from it, is the result of grief or other emotion, or of coughing or laughter.' Balzac's chemist tried to analyse his wife's tears. 'Tears,' said he cynically, 'what are tears? ... They contain some chloride of soda, some phosphate of lime, a little water, and that is all.'

But there is much in this life beyond a test-tube's analysis! Have you noticed the tears in the New Testament? Beginning as it does with the song of the angels over the Christ-Child, and ending with the triumph of the redeemed, it has been called the Book of Joy; but it would never minister to our hearts as it does, without its tears. To its early Greek readers, its shortest verse was its most surprising—rendered in our version: 'Jesus wept' (Jn 11[35]). That the Son of God, the Divine One, could be so human, was beyond belief.

By now, the scene is almost too familiar to us—the beloved Lazarus has died, and after considerable delay Jesus has arrived. He is met by the sisters Mary and Martha, and there in the garden beside the family tomb Jesus sheds tears. The tears of a strong man are always moving.

Our New Testament grants us still another glimpse. Making His way from this village of Bethany on another occasion, He beholds the City, and weeps. This time it is not *personal grief*, it is *national grief*.

Personal grief escapes none of us; but I doubt if there has ever been a century like this when men, women, and little children have known such national grief. Historians may pass over the hour when Sir Winston Churchill paid a brief visit to a particular place, typical of many, where a land-mine had fallen, but some will always remember it. He and General Ismay, his companion, found amidst devastated houses, a little group of strained and tired people trying to salvage their few possessions. Emotion welled up, and tears streamed down the face of the Leader of the nation. 'You see,' said an old lady standing amid the ruins, 'he really cares, he's crying.'

Millions today are refugees—one in every four, a child. I have looked at their pitiful little bundles; I have seen them crouched under rough bedouin tents on the hot stones of Jordan; I have seen them shelterless under the sky at the railway-station in Calcutta; I have met them trudging wearily along the endless roads of Europe.

Wherever life sets us down, there is no week, no day, no hour that does not bring tears to someone's eyes. Within the narrowest circle, there is a constant call for sympathy. In its richest content, that word means 'fellow-feeling'. It is a strong word, expressive of the attitude of our Lord.

In His tears, He steps down from the stained-glass window, and stands close beside us.

53

At the Lake of the Moon

THERE IS something fantastic about a colony of craftsmen and their families devoted to making bride-bangles at the Lake of the Moon. But when one knows about them, they make claims on one's sympathy in a very down-to-earth fashion.

Their craft goes back generations. When a Hindu girl becomes betrothed, she has the right to wear bangles cut from a conch shell. These are really her 'engagement ring', part of the elaborate ritual of her religion. To meet the need, craftsmen at Dacca in East Pakistan have developed their ancient skill to a high degree.

But a tragic up-rooting of these people took place in 1947, during the disturbances occasioned by Independence. Carrying what little they could, they found themselves part of the three million refugees that poured into Bengal. In all there were two hundred and sixty families devoted to cutting the white bangles from the shells. They settled in Chandanpuker—'The Lake of of the Moon'—fifteen miles north of Calcutta.

Lacking resources, they were soon in desperate straits. Their saws and other necessary tools were unbelievably primitive. It might seem to an outsider highly picturesque to ply such an ancient craft as bangle-making for brides at the Lake of the Moon, but the stern truth was that there were mouths to be fed. That was not easy. Clothes were of the simplest, and shelter of a temporary, fragile nature; but the torn-up families from the traditional setting were unorganized. When the Bengal

Refugee Service—a joint Church organization—looked into the situation, it did not like what it saw.

Something had to be done, and done quickly. And it is to the praise of this compassionate Christian Service that something of a practical nature has been started. A co-operative effort seemed the best way to put the colony on its feet. New sources of supply for conch shells had to be found, a workshop built to afford the craftsmen shelter, and to speed things up, a few modern electric cutting-machines have been installed. To make this possible, funds have been forthcoming from the churches—half as an outright gift, the remainder in the nature of a grant, to be paid off as a co-operative effort during the next fifteen years.

The word 'compassion' appears again and again in the New Testament. We read that when our Lord 'saw the crowds, He was moved with compassion' (Mt 9^{36}). It was no vague sentiment; as someone has observed, whenever Jesus was moved, He always *did* something. The word may not be often on our lips these days, but our Lord will not let us forget what it means. In the New Testament record, 'the word which is used for *moved with compassion (splagchnistheis)*' as Dr. William Barclay reminds us, 'is the strongest word for compassionate pity in the Greek language'.

54

A New Perspective

I AM SEEING the streets and skies from my own hills, in a new light. I've been abroad for a year—and it's one of the rewards of travel that the things of home are seen in a new perspective. That was what Alfred Noyes discovered, and set down, in *The Return of the Home-Born*.

> *All along the white chalk coast*
> > *The mist lifts clear.*
> *Wight is glimmering like a ghost*
> > *The ship draws near.*
> *Little inch-wide meadows,*
> > *Lost so many a day,*
> *The first time I knew you*
> > *Was when I turned away.*

G. K. Chesterton—master of paradox—was saying the same thing in the reply he gave to a friend who asked where he was going: 'I am going to see England. The only reason for going abroad is to see England.' He was not thinking, as was Noyes, of the delights of nature, the headlands misted over, the meadows, the villages, the little winding lanes, and all the dear things that pull at an Englishman's heart. Chesterton paid little attention to such—he was thinking more of the things of the mind—and the same rule applies. Our modern story-teller, Somerset Maugham, knows that. 'A few years ago,' said he, 'I offered a scholarship of four hundred pounds sterling a year, to enable a young writer to travel. I gave the scholarship because I thought—and still think—a writer should write about his own country. To do this successfully, he must leave it, for life in a foreign place enables him to see his home from a broader stand-point.'

Is this not why our young Master left the place He knew so well, and the people He knew so well, and went off into the Wilderness? At the very outset of His ministry that was to mean so much for the world, He needed a sense of perspective.

So do we all. We so easily become prisoners of the unimportant, so easily lose the big in consideration of the small, the vital in the trivial.

It was this that Paul had in mind when he prayed for his friends: 'It is my prayer that your love may be more and more rich in knowledge and all manner of insight, enabling you to have a sense of what is vital (Phil 1⁹, Moffatt). Isn't that beautifully put?

But how can we do this? A fine book is a help. When we have made the journey into the great North-West Frontier of India—through Dr Henry Holland's *Frontier Doctor*—we are bound to see some things differently when we return. And there is another way, as Earl Haig knew in exacting days. In a brief letter to his padre, he wrote: 'It was very difficult to keep going, and I am frequently asked how I managed to do it. Well, I can truly say that you were a great help to me in putting *things into their proper perspective on Sundays*!'

55

It's Tough!

I MET THEM as I went down the hill this morning—
a milling, eager bunch of small boys in club-colours
and shorts, carrying football boots. Two hours later
they would return, mud-bespattered, to play the game
all over again in verbal give-and-take. This is the
pattern of Saturday mornings just now. To call it 'a
beastlie furie', even 'a friendly kind of fight', not to
mention 'a bloody and murdering practice', would be
to offend these young devotees. They do not know,
much less care, that as early as 1314, there were com-
plaints of 'great uproar . . . from great *footballs* in the
fields of the public'. A few years later—in 1365—able-
bodied men, 'under pain of imprisonment' were clearly
warned against meddling 'in the hurling of stones,
loggatts [whatever they were], quoits, handball, *football*
or other vain games of no value'. Two centuries later,
one as roundly condemned the game as 'nothing but
beastlie furie and extreme violence, whereof proceedeth
hurte and consequently rancour and malice'. But the
menace was still present twenty years later. Philip
Stubbs wrote in his *Anatomie of Abuses* (lovely title):
'As concerning football playing, I protest unto you it
may rather be called a friendly kind of fight, than a
play or recreation; a bloody and murdering practice,
than a friendly sport or pastime. For doth not everyone
lie in wait for his adversary, seeking to overthrow him
and to pitch him on his nose?'

Not easily were rules devised to the satisfaction of
players and beholders, and to the greater safety of all.

Kingston upon Thames claims the invention of football, a thousand years or more ago. The doughty townsfolk fought off the marauding Danes. It happened on Shrove Tuesday, and for years on the anniversary of that notable victory, the townsfolk played their version of the game—from eleven in the morning till five in the afternoon. Kicking the ball through the town, the winning side (I will not call it a team) was the one to get the ball nearest an agreed spot by five. The *Daily News* report, as late as 1846, was delightfully vague on rules, satisfied to give but an impression of 'full-blooded football' in the best, or worst sense.

A few years earlier William Webb Ellis of Rugby School—as I was reminded a little while ago when I spotted a large plaque on the wall of the sports' field—'with a fine disregard for the rules of football as played in his time, first took the ball in his hands, and ran with it, thus originating the distinctive feature of the Rugby game'.

But it is a word of Oliver Wendell Holmes—stirred this morning, on meeting that eager bunch of boys—that is foremost in my mind: '*Truth is tough*: it is like a football: you may kick it about all day, but it remains round and full in the evening.' I like that. Once grasp that regarding the greatest truth revealed, and we need never be afraid for it. Why should we be? Truth cannot finally contradict truth—whether it comes through science or Scripture. *God does not contradict Himself. Truth is tough!*

56

Daily Bread

WHAT DO YOU see when you open your front door?
A pleasant bit of garden, a few trees, and distant
blue hills to lift the eyes, lie beyond mine. And something more now. In his book, Donald K. Faris says
with stabbing realism: 'Visualize a line from your front
door, made up of the hungry of the world. The line
goes out of sight over continent and ocean around the
world—25,000 miles—and returns to your front door.
On and on it stretches circling the globe not once,
twice or five times, but twenty-five, and there is no
one in the line but hungry, suffering humanity.'

It is a less pleasing prospect than garden, trees, and
hills; but I dare not disregard it with a shrug of the
shoulders. It's too real. And you and I are involved in
it. It is part of the painful pattern in which our lives
are set. 'The question of bread for myself,' as Dr
Berdyaev has said, 'is a material question, but the
question of bread for my neighbour, for everybody, is
a spiritual question.' It faces us every time we pray the
opening words of The Lord's Prayer—'*Our* Father . . .'.
It is implicit in the fact that we live among the 'haves'
of this world, and not among the pitiful 'have-nots'.
And nothing but geography has placed us—no least
merit of our own.

You and I must brace ourselves to see that line
stretching out from our front doors; and we must search
in our compassionate hearts, and our purses, to do
something about it. How can we ever again look out
without remembering it? It is not enough to throw

upon the State the total burden of what we see, and feel. It is good that we should do what we can to rouse the conscience of the State; but social action and personal responsibility belong together; as Christian individuals, we have each a response to make.

> *While some of my brothers*
> *In misery lie,*
> *I cannot pray 'Father',*
> *And pass them by.*
> *Of what use is doctrine,*
> *Or dogma, or creed,*
> *If I lack awareness*
> *Of my brothers' need?*

Those who make up that line are powerless to improve their own lot—they lack too much. While they do not live by bread alone, without bread they cannot live at all. The difference between life and death in Indonesia, Pakistan, Afghanistan may be the difference between a shining hoe and a piece of stick to cultivate the ground; the difference between a sparse crop and a sufficient one, a gift of new seed. You and I must send them these, through the Food and Agriculture Organization of the United Nations, and through the National Council of Churches—that exist to help us answer our prayer: '*Our Father.* . . . Hallowed be Thy Name. . . . Thy will be done in earth. . . . Give *us* this day our daily bread.'

57

The Present Generation

SOME PARSONS, parents, reporters seem not to know a verse in Ecclesiastes: 'Say not thou, *What is the cause that the former days were better than these?* For thou dost not consider wisely concerning this' (7^{10}).

It has become a fashion to lament the behaviour of modern youth—and evidence is not lacking to serve a doleful tale. 'The young people of today,' says one, in a generalizing tone, 'think of nothing but themselves. They have no reverence for parents or old age. They are impatient of restraint. They talk as if they knew everything, and what passes for wisdom with us is foolishness with them. As for the girls, they are forward and immodest, and unwomanly in speech, behaviour, and dress.'

But wait a moment! That judgement was not made this morning, though it sounds uncommonly like what we constantly hear. It was made by one Peter, a monk, in 1274! It belongs to those 'former years' which have become so out of focus, that it is the easiest thing to generalize. The simple truth is that those days were in many respects *no better than today, though perhaps no worse*. What we need is a sense of perspective, and a sense of fair play. For the damning judgement of modern youth that is so easy to make, is never the whole truth.

My neighbour looked over the hedge. She is a grandmother, living alone—silver-haired, quietly-spoken, Christian. 'I'll be away for a week,' she began. 'I wonder if you'd take in my mail and morning paper.'

Then she went on to explain her brief absence. 'I'm going down to my daughter's, to keep house.' Then out came the whole happy story. Each summer her daughter and her husband and teen-age trio—two lads, eighteen and twenty, and their sister—spend weeks at their beach-house; they are joined by young friends. Since there isn't room for all in the house, they bring tents and set them up on the lawn; and a jolly company they are, joining Peter with his accordion, Wally with his guitar, as well as Dad at the grass-cutting, and Mum at the house-keeping. Later, while the good weather lasts, those who must, go to and from work.

A week or so ago the young folk felt it was time they said their thanks in a special way. So back—the summer ended—they sprang a surprise-party on their host and hostess. It took them completely unawares, though their own young folk were 'in the know'. After a jolly evening, they served a sumptuous supper—sandwiches, savouries, pavlovas, cakes, coffee, and tea—insisting the while that mother should stay out of the kitchen. But that was not all—at a suitable juncture, one of the lads made a little speech, and to their good summer host and hostess handed an envelope. It contained a receipt for a week's stay for both of them at a private hotel a hundred-odd miles distant—chosen, booked, and paid for by the teen-agers themselves.

And when my neighbour made her simple request of me, she was off down to 'hold the fort'.

Youth may be decadent in many of its doings today—but that isn't the whole truth—*let us hear the other side, too.*

58

Private Rainbows

FOR WEEKS I have been scanning the skies; and this morning I had my reward—a lovely shower fell. One could literally smell the garden lapping it up. And when the sun burst through, there was a glorious rainbow. I don't wonder that poets go into ecstasies, when ordinary gardeners like myself are moved. Wordsworth exclaimed:

> *My heart leaps up when I behold*
> *A rainbow in the sky;*
> *So was it when my life began;*
> *So is it now I am a man;*
> *So be it when I shall grow old,*
> *Or let me die!*

A rainbow's message is *one of Hope*. And from childhood to old age we must have that.

Looking across the valley I felt glad that there remain areas of life beyond man's power to make or spoil. So many things have been changed—the wandering river harnessed, the hillside denuded of its forest; the atom studied and split. But nothing has happened to the rainbow; it remains exactly as when Noah came forth from the Ark, to face the renewal of the erstwhile flooded earth. As I thought of this, I found myself unashamedly echoing my friend, Dr Leslie Church: 'It is good to see the glory of the rainbow . . . and to know that there is something in it that cannot be caught within the limits of a laboratory experiment, or what we call physical life.'

It makes no difference whether, in imagination, I look at Noah's rainbow arching the heavens, or my own. In each case, *God put it there.* And come what will, our human hope remains in God. There are some things that for all our modern cleverness, we cannot create for ourselves.

When I speak of 'my rainbow', in relation to Noah's, it is not to be egotistical. Recent study of atmospherics reveals that every rainbow that blesses any one of us, is a private rainbow. 'Since each observer,' says the modern expert, 'sees a rainbow arch around a specific point in the sky opposite the sun from its own position, *no two people ever see the same bow.*'

Amazing! And full of spiritual significance!

The hope which God sets in your sky is not necessarily the same as He sets in mine. In His own supreme way He matches our heart's need. He is not condemned to do things in the mass; nothing is more clearly revealed in Jesus' uncovering of His divine nature—He is the God of one sparrow, one wayside flower, one rainbow!

So with new wonder now, the words of Ecclesiasticus (43[13]) stir my heart: '*Look on the rainbow, and bless Him who made it!*'

59

Giving Ourselves Away

A CHILDREN'S fancy-dress party can be fun. I
found myself involved a while ago. As the date
approached I began to think about my costume. I
remembered having seen a jovial representation of the
Michelin Tyre man worn by a university student in
the Annual Rag. I sought out the office of the agent,
and came quickly to the point: 'Could I hire the outfit?'
'Certainly, Madam.' 'I suppose I could get into it,' I
queried. 'Surely, Madam.' 'And what fee do you
charge?' 'Oh, that's free. Just give us your address,
and the date, and we'll see that you get it.'

I came out into the street jubilant about my little
secret. But when a week later I arrived home for tea on
the date of the party, it hadn't arrived. Presently, a
lorry backed in, and a man knocked at the door. 'Where
do you want this?' he asked, with a sweep of his hand
towards his load, a packing-case nearly the size of a
piano. 'Oh, round the back,' I answered blithely.
'Have you a man about the place who could help me?'
Then the family set on to me: 'To think you're going
to a party,' they said, 'in a thing a man can't lift!' But
it wasn't as bad as that, when I had wrenched off the
lid—the timber of the case was an inch thick.

Then came the fun of getting into the thing. In
three parts—the legs in the likeness of a series of small
tyres, went on like a pair of pants with braces; next
came the body, larger tyres also made of canvas
whitened over; then the head-piece. To the weighty,
suffocating whole, I added black slippers, and decided

never to speak a word while I was in it. I also removed my watch and dress-ring, lest I be identified. Then I sent a little note to the leader of the party—carefully worded—saying that I was sorry that they wouldn't *see me* at the party after all.

Later—having donned my outfit at a friend's home near the place of gathering—I bounced my way in among the youngsters. And for the next two hours I was at the mercy of them. I can't remember a party when I worked so hard; and inside it got hotter and hotter. The leader read my apology to accompanying moans of disappointment, and among the parents present arose immediate speculation as to what illness could have overwhelmed me. And then, suddenly, my secret was out. I had kept silence for two hours, removed watch and ring, but I had forgotten *my double-jointed thumb*! From the far end of the hall one lively spirit raised the cry, 'I know who it is—look at her thumb!' And from all quarters, a bevy of youngsters set on me. Perhaps I deserved it.

So unexpectedly we give ourselves away. I thought of Peter caught unawares. Three times over came his test while his Lord stood Trial—and the third was final: 'Thou also art one of His followers—*thy speech betrayeth thee*!' (Mt 26[73]). Peter's Galilean accent, like the Arabic spoken in those parts today, had peculiarities; *but it was so much of himself, he hadn't thought of that.* And that is how it is—our discipleship depends far less on the length of our prayers, our recitation of the Creed, and the loudness of our testimony, than upon the little, unconscious, natural things about us that others notice.

60

Many Members—One Body

IN THE nature of things I come off better than my friend who is a teacher of music. Between my pleasant book-lined study and her music-room is a large sliding door, the work of a local craftsman. It serves us well, though nobody pretends that it excludes every sound. I have no idea what my muted typewriter sounds like; I know only that from time to time my mind is set off on a fresh and wholly unexpected line, because of what comes through to me.

At coffee-break this morning I questioned my friend about something I had overheard, and she brought in the music for me to examine—a dainty minuet by Boccherini.

Luigi Boccherini, I learned, was born in Tuscany about two hundred years ago. He received his early lessons from his father, a double-bass player; but went on to compose and to perform under royal patronage in Madrid. He composed oratorios, cantatas and motets, operas, and a score of symphonies. But where his name lives today, it is chiefly as a master of chamber-music.

To my surprise, I was able to tell my friend a story about him that she didn't know. The Prince of the royal house derived much joy from music. But one night as he sat in the music-room with Boccherini and two others, a crisis arose. On this occasion, the Prince's part was a very small one, and he grew impatient as his master of music plucked away at his 'cello, and the second violin and viola played on. He began to pour scorn on the new composition. Boccherini was in no mood to be insulted, and he spoke up courageously: 'If your Highness will but listen to the other instruments, he will find that his part blends, and therefore is of equal importance.' At that the Prince's patience deserted him altogether, and picking up the little musician, he rushed to the door of the music-room and threw him out.

But Boccherini was right—what he said was a simple, lasting law of life that a prince as well as the humblest person who draws breath must learn.

With our varying gifts, we have to hammer out the art of working together. When—coffee ended—my friend returned to her work, I fell to thinking about this. Paul was very strong on the word 'together'—'God,' he wrote, 'hath quickened us *together* . . .' (Eph 2⁵). He wrote about 'Being knit *together* in love . . .' (Col 2²), and about 'Striving *together* for the faith of the Gospel' (Phil 1²⁷). This recurring emphasis arose out of the difficulties Paul knew in the early Church. And who can claim, even in this day of the World Council of Churches, when we sit together in great conferences, that we have resolved it at the local level? In the Church which is the Body of Christ, we have each to learn how to honour a fellow-member—not in spite of his differences, but because of his differences. Paul reminds us that we are *'many members, but one body'*. Says he: 'The eye cannot say unto the hand, I have no need of thee; nor again the head to the feet, I have no need of you' (1 Cor 12²¹).

It is not without significance that this leads up to Paul's great chapter on Love (1 Cor 13)! For Love is the heart of the matter still.

61

Problems on Legs

I POPPED INTO my favourite coffee-shop, and as I took my seat at one of the little tables a snatch of conversation reached me. The word 'problem', I couldn't help noticing, was repeated several times.

'Problem' has come to be one of our most over-worked words; scarcely a conversation proceeds without it. We have the problem of the pre-school age, the problem of the adolescent, the problem of the worker, the problem of the retired, the problem of the aged, the problem of the refugee. Is psychology responsible for the fact that we have become so 'problem-minded'? Or is it that in our approach to people we have grown impersonal? A youth, in our judgement, is a problem; so is a coloured worker; and an unmarried mother; and an old woman with nowhere to go. But first of all, these are people—*not problems on legs*.

'The study of mankind,' says G. M. Trevelyan, 'does not resemble the study of the physical properties of atoms, or the life-history of animals. If you find out about one atom you have found out about all atoms, and what is true about one robin, is roughly true of the habits of all robins. But the life history of one man, or even of many individual men, will not tell you the life history of other men. . . . Men are too complicated, too spiritual, too various.'

There was something very real in the approach of our Master. 'Well did He know what was in human nature,' said one of His close observers (Jn 2²⁵, Moffatt). He knew the latent good in bad people, and the secret flaws in good people—but to Him they were always people, not problems.

Too often to dub a person a 'problem' is to dismiss him as impossible. Abstractions are well enough for the study and lecture-room, but for the common give-and-take of life, we need something warmer, more patient, and more human. Mr Perry Burgess, Director of the American Leprosy Foundation, underlines this. In *Born of the Years*, he tells of a day when he stood with a doctor at the gates of a leprosarium in Korea. He saw one of the inmates point to a boy among the throng outside, pleading for his admission; and heard the answer that there was no room. 'But,' she replied, 'he is not nearly as bad as the others. They are like me, finished, no hope—he is not finished.'

'Yes, I know all that,' said the doctor, with torture in his voice, 'but what can we do? There is no room.' There was a dreadful silence for a moment, and then the old, paralysed, ravaged face turned up imploringly. 'I will go, doctor,' she said. 'He may have my place. He wants the food and a place to sleep. He must have medicine you will give him. Some day he may be well again.'

'You!' said the doctor. 'You would go out again to sleep in the fields or in the streets? In heaven's name, why will you do this?' The silence was long. The gaze of the old broken thing went slowly from doctor to boy, to the gates of the leprosarium and back to the doctor. Her words were scarcely audible: 'Because, doctor—he is my son!'

Too Big to be Small

A RADIOGRAM is a joy. Among those whose art I admire, I have a lovely record of Dame Edith Evans speaking Shakespearean Sonnets.

While visiting New York, Dame Edith was reported as saying: 'I hear that some of your young actors go to psychiatrists to find out, as they say, their "real selves". Rubbish! They're skipping life. They're shirking. *Good actors don't go about thinking of themselves all the time.*'

Much of the tension that we know today is caused by each putting himself at the centre of the picture. The plain truth is that we were none of us fashioned to reach satisfaction that way. Part of the technique of handling life lies in some activity that forces us *to look away from ourselves*. Thus closely tied to our necessity is *Worship*.

Occasionally we hear a plea for Christian Worship based on a need to keep the Church going; the truth is rather that we need to keep ourselves going. We are so fashioned that if we fail to lift our eyes to One higher than ourselves and our earth-bound purposes, we perish in the most real depths of personality. Worship is something more than a shallow expression of preference —something that we like to do because we've been brought up to it, or because we are temperamentally unsuited to golf, or hiking, or digging up dandelions in the back lawn on Sunday mornings. 'To Worship', is to do something too big to be small; it is, as William Temple says, 'to quicken the conscience by the Holiness of God; to purge the imagination by the Beauty of God; to open the heart to the Love of God; to devote the will to the Purpose of God.'

Some of us at times find this difficult. Jeremiah had to live in a less complicated age than ours. There were no psychiatrists then, in elegant consulting-rooms. Jeremiah went to Worship; but his ego marched in right away and took up a position in the clamorous forefront. Turn up the record, and hear his cry: 'O Lord, remember *me*, and visit *me*, and avenge *me* of *my* persecutors; take *me* not away in Thy long-suffering; and know that for Thy sake *I* have suffered reproach. Why is *my* pain perpetual, and *my* wound incurable which refuseth to be healed?' (Jer 15$^{15, 18}$).

But we have uncomfortably fresh memories of our own self-importance.

How shall we live fully if we fail to lift up our eyes to the Creator of all, the lasting Father of our spirits? How shall we forget ourselves unless we lose ourselves in His on-going purpose for this universe which holds nuclear energy of unguessed potential, a disputed boundary in Berlin, the matchless beauty of a Shake-spearean Sonnet, the song of a little child, the challenge of a hungry neighbour.

Worship—by derivation 'a recognition of worth'—is that act by which we ascribe absolute worth to God, and give Him the glory due unto His Name. Reinhold Niebuhr sets down in a sentence what some of us are distressingly slow to learn: '*The Worship of a perfectly Holy God saves us from premature satisfaction with ourselves.*'

63

A Miracle

As young Dr Gray lay in his bed up in the mountains during his prolonged illness, his thoughts were all of his people of Indonesia. His service to them for the moment was at an end. Little did he know that they were together on the edge of a miracle.

From his bed, the sight of the villagers shearing the odd sheep with clumsy scissors, and throwing away the wool as useless, set going a request to his homeland for advice. The young New Zealander could not bear the thought of such waste. In a land of dire poverty, every least commodity demanded to be utilized.

Once the need was communicated, offers of advice were not slow; but it was a chance meeting of a country friend on a visit to town that changed everything. In a busy Auckland street she unexpectedly encountered an expert in wool-weaving. 'You're just the person we need,' came the greeting. And in no time, stepping aside from the pressure of hurrying passers-by, the situation in Bandung was shared, and the address given.

So it came about that at the end of April, Mrs Kathleen O'Reilly—an Anglican, associated with the nearby Methodist Church—left New Zealand by air, on a three month's assignment, to Bandung. Using the hospital as a base, she hoped she might teach wool-shearing, carding, spinning, and weaving to the patients, the villagers, and any others interested. She hoped also to be able to explore the possibilities of marketing such products.

It was not easy to get away, but friends eager to

stand behind the venture came forward with offers of help. Assured that her husband and two children—ten and thirteen—would be in good hands, Mrs O'Reilly set off. In the brief interval a good deal of interest had been created by radio and television interviews. As a result, gifts of looms and spinning-wheels began to come in. Once the preparations for such an unexpected venture began to take shape, Mrs O'Reilly herself approached wool and carpet firms, and collected many donations.

In time—realizing the far-reaching possibilities of the good neighbourly task to which she had put her experience and energy—she set up at her hospital base. But more was needed; and soon she was giving demonstrations in village squares, and in the annual Fair among the crowds of Bandung. And the news spread. People who had formerly thrown away the wool, looked now upon the results of this newcomer's skill, as upon a miracle. 'Everywhere,' says the doctor, 'her enthusiasm and skill caught the imagination of the people. Markets have been found for the finished articles, and the Indonesian Government has been so impressed, that they have asked her to stay a month longer at their expense, and tour in Sumatra. To date,' the doctor rejoices to add, 'the Wool Project far surpasses our wildest dreams.' And what the end will be, no one can tell.

Love and skill can still work miracles!

64

The Last Word

CONSIDERABLE expectation on the part of the Master and students of King's College, Brisbane, awaited Sir Edgeworth David when he arrived to speak. The famous geologist was soon sharing his experiences in Antarctica. But it was an unexpected witness to his faith, that of all his learned lecture will live longest with some who listened. He spoke of the ice and snow stretching endlessly—their very immensity dwarfing for him his sense of human significance. But that was not all. Breaking in upon that mood, he had to confess, suddenly six words took charge: '*I am a child of God!*'

Antarctic ice and snow remain outside the gaze of most; but the same sense of insignificance crowds in upon us from other aspects of Nature. The Psalmist experienced this out under the great stars: 'When I consider Thy heavens, the work of Thy fingers, the moon and the stars, which Thou has ordained; What is man, that Thou art mindful of him: and the son of man that Thou visitest him?' (Ps 8[3-4]). One will describe him as 'a highly developed vertebrate, a more or less successful ape, who has worsted his competitors in the struggle for existence'. But the Psalmist, even in his early day, came to be sure of more—man, said he, is the centre of God's creation, care, and love: *He made me, He is mindful of me, He visiteth me.* 'He healeth the broken in heart . . . He telleth the number of the stars' (Ps 147[3-4]).

As our knowledge of the world in which we live

grows greater, the insignificance of the individual for many grows more real. The conception of the universe, unbelievably vast, paralyses the imagination. We see so many more stars than were visible to the Psalmist's naked eye; our telescopes grow greater and greater, probing farther and ever farther. Those points of light desolating the mind with their mystery, burn into many of us a sense of nothingness.

In broad daylight the age and size and complexity of the world comes home to us more and more. 'Our earth,' says Dr Roger Pilkington, in our day, 'is certainly a handsome mass of rocky materials, but its size in relation to the rest of the universe is ludicrously small. It trundles along through space, swinging round the giant Sun in an orbit more than ninety million miles in radius, spinning as it goes. It is only one of a family of several planets, and our Sun itself is in turn only one among thousands of millions of stars roughly spread out in the galaxy which we ingenuously call the "Milky Way".'

Put away the telescope and the latest revelation of science, and this same sense of insignificance strikes some of us in intimate nearness. Said one aware of it suddenly: 'I felt like a fly crawling on the score of the Fifth Symphony.' But for the man, the woman, among us who will pause to hear the voice of Him who talked about sparrows, and lilies of the field, of one son, one sheep, one coin, there is much more—a revealed relationship with the Father. The last word is not with the snowy spaces, the stars, the spinning earth, the intimate beauties of Nature—the last word is with religion: '*I am a child of God!*'

65

Unchanging Centre

THESE ARE days of continual change—hard, perhaps, on old folk. Off and on, through my upgrowing years in Nelson, I visited a little wooded hill, reputed to be the geographic centre of New Zealand. There was a plaque to assure us. Imagine the raised eyebrows this morning, on opening the paper, to be confronted with the bold headline:

CENTRE OF NEW ZEALAND CHANGES

An officer of the Department of Scientific and Industrial Research geophysical survey, with computer calculations, it seems, has decided that the true centre is miles distant in the Spooner Range.

Nothing, of course, can be done about it—in the light of new knowledge we must just get used to it—the plaque must be moved and the new centre marked. We can go on—if a little less confident about some externals.

At the heart of things, where most of all one lives, happily there is no question of new knowledge creating a like disturbance. In my early, eager teens, I discovered the truth of a scholar's words: 'The essence of the world's standard is that it sets self at the centre; the essence of the Christian standard is that it sets *Christ in the centre.*'

His birth, life, death, and resurrection are essential to any understanding of the universe. New scientific knowledge has done much to shatter confidence in a number of long-accepted centres; it is not surprising that many about us are bewildered. The little snug world they believed in, has gone for ever—earth has become a mounting-ground for capsules into outer-space. Human history has taken on new dimensions. *But still at the centre of it*—if it is to make sense—*is Jesus Christ*, the only begotten Son of God. When credit has been given all the great leaders and thinkers, Dr Fitchett is right: 'One name alone is stamped on the brow of the hurrying centuries, and it is the name of Jesus Christ.' His position is eternally at the centre, where the spirits of men and women out-reach, where questions about God, and life, and human significance, and a thousand others are asked. Is the universe friendly? Has it a deep meaning? Can lasting peace be realized between warring factions? Is happiness a will-o-the-wisp? Is there a way to surmount folly and failure, and to forgive human sin?

God's answer at the centre is '*Jesus Christ, the same yesterday, today and for ever*'—not a manifesto, much less a mandate, a radiant and sublime personality (Heb 13[8]). Nothing that the centuries have done, or with expanding knowledge, can do, can change Him; for as Dr Whale states superbly in our day: 'It is God Himself, person-ally present and redeemingly active, who comes to meet men in this Jesus of Nazareth.' In Him life finds its centre, and sin its defeat.

66

Keeping it Up

L ENT DOESN'T mean much to many. It gets its
name from *lengten-tide*, a Saxon term for Spring; by
degrees the two words became shortened to the one
with which we are familiar. Stretching from Ash
Wednesday to Easter Eve—of which the forty week-
days were early devoted to fasting and penitence—it
serves to remind us of our Lord's temptation in the
Wilderness.

Properly approached and observed, it is a most
valuable experience, though no amount of fish added
to our menu, or beef deleted from it, will result in a
properly kept Lent: it is much more than that. In
earlier centuries, of course, that wasn't a bad place at
which to start. There is a document extant belonging
to the fourteenth century—dated the thirty-first year
of the reign of King Edward the Third—which records
sums paid out for fish for the Royal Household: fifty
pounds for nine thousand red herrings; twelve pounds
for three thousand and fifty white herrings; six pounds
for two barrels of sturgeon; twenty-one pounds five
shillings for thirteen hundred stock-fish (whatever they
were); thirteen shillings and ninepence for eighty-nine
congers; and twenty marks for three hundred and
twenty mulwells (whatever they were).

Great gastronomic feats were a feature of earlier
centuries—and to fast was never easy. One remembers
the Percy's breakfast. The incredible order reads:
'Breakfast for my Lord and Lady *during Lent*—a loaf of
bread in trenchers, two manchets, two small white

loaves, a quart of beer, a quart of wine, two pieces of salt fish, six baconn'd herring, four white herring, or a dish of sprats.' Quite a breakfast at any time!

No wonder Robert Herrick, the little parson—turning his back on court and great house—found himself going much deeper for the meaning of Lent:

> *'Is this a Fast, to keep*
> *The larder lean,*
> *And clean*
> *From fat of veals and sheep?*
>
> *Is it to quit the dish*
> *Of flesh, yet still*
> *To fill*
> *The platter high with fish?'*
>
> *'No,' he answers,*
> *'It is to fast from strife,*
> *From old debate,*
> *And hate:*
> *To circumcise thy life.*
>
> To show a heart grief-rent;
> To starve thy sin,
> Not bin:
> And that's to keep thy Lent.'

It still is. Discipline could well begin with a tightening of the belt, but it must not stop there.

67

A Mighty 'If'

W<small>E ARE</small> constantly urging each other to be realistic, but few of us have the courage of Paul. He hangs all that life means on a mighty 'If'—'*If* Christ be not risen, then is our preaching vain, and your faith is also vain' (1 Cor 15[14]).

It is not enough that a young Man should have grown up in Nazareth, should in time have put up the shutters of His carpenter's shop to be an itinerant preacher, should have extended His hands in healing, should have instructed twelve to carry on when His own brief earthly adventure was finished, and at the end—with words of forgiveness on His lips—have died upon a Cross.

These things were important, of course; but not enough. If at last, all was swallowed up in Death—all the fine words that walked up and down in men's minds, all the brotherly gestures, the outgoing compassion—then, indeed, all was lost. And Paul himself was a fool in spending his body's strength, and the best thought of his schooled mind, declaring Him Lord of Life.

But Paul had faced all these possibilities and—lacking the Gospel records of the Resurrection that support our faith—had come, by all the rules of honest reckoning, to an unwavering certainty that Christ had risen from the dead. Assured of that, all things else fell into place for him—that was the one central truth. And it still is. 'All the evidence of the New Testament,' says Dr J. S. Whale, in his *Christian Doctrine*, 'goes to show that the burden of the good news or gospel was not "Follow this

Teacher and do your best", but *Jesus and the Resurrection*. You cannot take that away from Christianity without radically altering its character and destroying its very identity. It is the presupposition explicit and implicit of every chapter in the New Testament.'

That the Gospel records vary, in some of the details of what took place, only strengthens the case. If the four evangelists and Paul had set out to fabricate a story, they would have taken, I submit, far greater pains to see that their reports agreed in every line and detail. But they were men so carried away by the facts as they knew them, that they did not give a moment's thought to discrepancies. That is how it always is with a true witness. Reporting the battle of Waterloo, Wellington declared that it started at a certain time, Blücher reported a different hour; but the discrepancy in no way altered the fact that the battle was fought and won. So when the men who gave us the gospels came to set down what was for them the most amazing victory, each spoke out of his own experience. They were different types of men, they saw events from various angles, they selected out of a mass of evidence what most appealed.

And today, the one central fact stands as certain to us as ever to Paul and to those who lived through the first Easter:

> *He is not here: Love with its dying breath*
> *Has burst the bonds of Death. . .!*

68

No Sullen Saints

W ONDERFULLY telling can be a sentence spoken at the right time! Sister Mary Sealey, Methodist Deaconess among the Maori people, has just shared with me some words she can never forget, and has given me permission to pass them on. They were spoken to her by the Rev. A. J. Seamer, C.M.G., senior superintendent of Home and Maori Missions, retired and confined much to his bed. 'It was my first big assignment, you might say,' said Sister Mary, recalling that moment. 'I was off to visit some of the people. He spoke to me a few last words as I went in to see him just before I left: "*I don't say God go with you—but go with God.*" I've not heard any of the other workers ever speak of having heard the same thing. He didn't explain what he meant—he didn't need to. What a strength those words were then,' finished Sister Mary, 'and still are.'

Not all of us as quickly see the difference between choosing our own way and asking God's company in it, and giving ourselves over trustfully to going His way. And there is a world of difference.

God's way is no poor pale thing of resignation, but an experience of rejoicing and wonder. Whatever small satisfaction one's own will might bring, God's will is bound to be a thousand times more rewarding. I can understand how to some this seems merely a pious utterance; experience alone can prove it otherwise. Life is found to be either an ageless undertaking of largeness and greatness and light, or a small day-to-day expression of self-service.

Once one grasps this, there is no longer any real conflict in one's thoughts and plans, when one hushes one's heart to pray those wonderful words of The Lord's Prayer: 'Thy will be done in earth. . . .' No longer need one be involved in the petty dilemma in which a character in Cronin's story, *The Keys of the Kingdom*, found himself. 'He entered the pro-cathedral, an echoing vastness of beauty and silence,' says the author reverently. 'Undaunted, he marched toward the high altar. There he knelt and fiercely, with unshaken valour, prayed: "Oh, Lord, *for once*—not Thy will but mine, be done!"'

How refreshing to embrace the implications of those words Sister Mary Sealey has travelled with these many days—a simple distillation of the Covenant prayer: 'I am no longer my own, but Thine. Put me to what Thou wilt, rank me with whom Thou wilt; put me to doing, put me to suffering; let me be employed for Thee or laid aside for Thee, exalted for Thee or brought low for Thee; let me be full, let me be empty; let me have all things, let me have nothing; I freely and heartily yield all things to Thy pleasure and disposal . . . *Amen.*'

69

For the Thirsty

IT IS NOT easy for those of us set under a kindly sky, where showers fall gently and often, to understand the importance of water. Life has treated us so generously. The torment of thirst is missing altogether from the lines of our poet who writes lyrically:

> *Water is a lovely thing,*
> *Dark and ripply in a spring,*
> *Black and quiet in a pool,*
> *In a puddle brown and cool:*
> *In a river blue and gay,*
> *In a raindrop silver grey;*
> *In a fountain flashing white,*
> *In a dew-drop crystal bright. . . .*

Our Lord's words about 'a cup of cold water' never come alive for some of us. Still there are large areas of the earth's surface where the assuaging urgency of that simple injunction means the difference between life and death. An early church-record has lately turned up in Boulder, Western Australia. Strange transactions have from time immemorial taken place at church bazaars—we could all tell tales—but few, if any of us, have been called to spare a moment's thought for the primary concern of the people of Boulder. Sixty years ago the Church Trust, it is recorded, raised ten pounds *by the sale of rain-water*. Those words of our Lord must have been full of significance in Boulder. And, of course, they are still in many parts. We forget sometimes that water is more than the stuff of lyrical poetry, or even the 'colourless transparent tasteless scentless compound of oxygen and hydrogen, in its liquid state convertible by heat into steam, and by cold into ice—H_2O', that the young student in the science-laboratory knows.

A short time ago a plane flying from Nairobi was forced down by engine-trouble in the bush-country. Nowhere in those unknown spaces could the distressed passengers see any signs of human habitation. Their sole hope was to be spotted by planes sent out in search of them. Sizing up their situation, they spent their precious energies gathering stones, to set out on the parched ground in large letters their most urgent need, WATER !

'*My soul thirsteth for God,*' cried the Psalmist, '*for the living God.*'

Bible lands were parched lands, even more than now when attempts at water-conservation are being made. Still, surrounded by waterless deserts, rivers get swallowed up in sands, and dried up completely in fierce heat.

So it was something very real that our Lord meant when He talked about giving 'living water'. It was a tremendous claim—to be able permanently to satisfy the soul. But He makes that claim with calm assurance: '*Whosoever drinketh of the water that I shall give him, shall never thirst*' (Jn 4^{14}).

Many of us living on the unexamined surface of existence, do not recognize our deep-down dissatisfaction as thirst—and that to assuage it means the difference between life and death.

70

Point of View

I IMAGINED I KNEW every field and tree on the pleasant winding road between my home and the airport; but today I made a discovery. Instead of travelling in my little car, with my eyes on the road, my view of the undulating countryside hindered by hedges, I clambered up into a seat in the airport bus, and *looked right over them*. That gave me a refreshingly new point-of-view. I found myself saying over half-forgotten words:

> *Looking with stranger's eyes*
> *From the windows of the hump-backed bus*
> *That between air-port and station*
> *Lackadaisically plies. . . .*
> *Here's strangeness: gardens trim*
> *With flower-frills and leafy green;*
> *Bright windows, gaily prim. . . .*
> *And glossy as new colour-prints. . . .*
> *As we look upon Paris and Rome,*
> *See, with delighted surprise,*
> *The smiling suburbs of home!*

It is an exciting world in which such things happen! But there is a yet richer discovery waiting to be made. J. B. Phillips renders a verse in Paul's Epistle to the Colossians (1⁹), 'We are asking God that you may see things, as it were, from *His point of view*.' A startling prayer—it seems at first presumptuous, if not impossible. How can any mortal creature see things from God's point-of-view?

And yet would Paul have prayed such a prayer if it were not possible? Granted the gift of spiritual insight and understanding, he had no doubt about it. Those to whom he wrote—though they had cast off their old pagan ways—knew in actual fact that there was still a great deal of difference between their point-of-view and God's. In Jesus Christ they had seen expressed, beyond question, God's point-of-view. 'Call down fire on the unco-operative Samaritans?' '*No! for the Son of Man is not come to destroy men's lives, but to save them.*' That is God's point-of-view! 'Sell a flask of precious ointment in the market for three hundred pence?' *No! Pour it out in Love, till the place is filled with its fragrance!* That is God's point-of-view! 'Look after number one; build yourself better barns, settle down and be comfortable?' '*No! He that saveth his life shall lose it; and he that loseth his life for My sake shall find it!*' That is God's point-of-view!

There can never be any doubt about these things any more. Yet for twenty centuries some have gone on as though they never existed. No wonder our world is sick. We still want to call down fire—atom fire; we still want to sell for a profit, instead of give; we still want to make ourselves cosy, instead of pouring out our energies in one glorious continuous adventure, called The Kingdom of God!

71

Jack-in-the-box

WHILE GUEST of Queen Salote, I tried to find out about Falcon Island. The Tongans call it Fonuafo'ou, meaning New Land, though Sir Harry Luke's nickname, 'Jack-in-the-Box Island', is a good deal more descriptive.

Not many of us have been at the birth of an island. Accompanied by flaming festoons of lava hissing into the sea, the sight is a fascinating one.

H.M.S. *Falcon*, cruising in Tongan waters in 1865, first suspected that something surprising was taking place. And she had the honour of providing a name when it was needed for a new island that seamen and cartographers had somehow to deal with.

Twelve years later, when the *Sappho* sailed that way, no island was to be seen. All that was visible was smoke rising from the sea. Eight years later, the island seems to have decided it was time to reappear, and suddenly, one dawn, there it was again. Within twelve months it was two miles long and three hundred feet above sea-level at its highest point. But its stay was brief; five years later it had completely gone. In 1894, it made a further appearance, and in time became a considerable island. Then suddenly it disappeared once more. By 1927 it had reappeared—to reach its greatest recorded height of four hundred and seventy-five feet, about the height of the dome of St Paul's Cathedral. By 1949, those interested in its behaviour scanned the horizon, once more in vain.

And still it keeps up its unreliable tricks; no one can

predict with any certainty when it will be visible, and when it will be hidden beneath the sea.

This strange little island, fittingly nick-named, reminds one of a word of Paul's. 'We are proud of you,' he wrote to some of his friends, *'proud of the stedfastness and faith you display'* (2 Thess 1⁴, Moffatt). And I could as gladly address the same word to many of my own friends. The old word 'steadfast' (or dropping the 'a') is not commonly used these days, yet what a lovely quality it is, in a friend, in a family, a club, a workplace, a church! Said Pitt, of Dundas, that unobtrusive Scot: 'Dundas is no orator; he is not even a speaker—*but Dundas will go out with you in any weather.*'

Jack-in-the-Box characters doubtless add to the surprise of life; but dependability that the New Testament calls 'stedfastness' is beyond price. When Dr Tittle, from his famous Evanston pulpit, declared the judgement of God on war and injustice, and His blessing on patience, tolerance, and mercy, some took sides against him. But one man went to the heart of the matter: 'Years ago,' said he, 'when my wife died, and my world fell to pieces, and I walked all night along the lake shore, my minister, without my ever asking him, walked all night beside me. He can say whatever he believes, and I will listen.'

Dependability goes as deep as that!

72

A New Thought

DRIVING THROUGH Lithgow one morning with my friends, the Rev. Harold and Mrs Doust, some lines from *Everyday Religion* sprang to my lips:

> *Give us this day our daily bread,*
> *we pray,*
> *And give us likewise, Lord, our*
> *daily thought.*
> *That our poor souls may strengthen*
> *as they ought,*
> *And starve not on the husks of*
> *yesterday.*

Outside the church, for the benefit of passers-by like ourselves, was a board bearing the church's name, and below THOUGHT FOR THE DAY—*and the space was empty!* It was perhaps unfortunate that we passed just then— it might have been the interval at the changing of the board—but there it was.

Ought there to be any day that lacks a new thought? There are times, it has to be admitted, when our comfort is shattered by a thought; but we must face it. 'The Son of Man,' says Dr T. R. Glover, 'comes in queer shapes and forms, in new duties, and I think particularly *in the distasteful duty of thinking things over again.*'

Yesterday's thought won't do. It has to be re-thought —to come alive in each new situation. This responsibility is laid on each of us. 'God hath not given us the spirit of fear; but of power, and of love, and of *a sound mind*' (2 Tim 1⁷). Dr Glover underlines this essential:

'If we are effectively to preach Christ, we must secure that He is not in the minds of thinking people associated with antiquated scholarship or discredited science . . . I venture to predict that no real and permanent revival of religion is to be looked for where science and scholarship are ignored or refused.'

It strikes one as pathetic that so many Christian people will spend pocket-money on a plethora of newspapers, journals, paper-jackets, 'who-dunnits', and 'bosom-claspers', and a great deal on Wireless, TV, and films, and will never in years buy themselves a modern book on religion. Today there are glorious things to be had, written in the language of the lay-person, relevant to the world situation. It is not enough to ask of our religion that we be cheered and comforted—we must also be challenged. *'Brace up your minds, then,'* says the New Testament (1 Peter 1¹³, Moffatt). Daily bread is not one whit more important than daily thought.

73

Known and Unknown

WHEN I FIRST heard that little Japanese Christian, Kagawa, speak, he was scarcely known—now men call him a saint.

News of his death sent thousands the world round to thank God for what he had been able to accomplish.

Born of a rich father and a 'geisha girl' within sound of temple bells, he was bereft of both parents by the age of four. In loneliness, he was hurried off to his father's wife in a family mansion, to pick up an education. He became in time a brilliant student; but that was not to mean ease. He was cast off by his family for his Christian faith. With T.B. in both lungs, partially blind, and with an indifferent heart history, scorned, despised, he made his bed in the slums with the sick, the syphilitic, the starving. But he became a very brother in Christ to multitudes; he became a deep scholar, a social revolutionary, a doctor of philosophy, founder of trades unions, poet, author of many books—Kagawa!

When this has been said, there yet remains something else—and it was said beautifully and unforgettably by his own daughter, Umeko, serving with the World Council of Churches in Geneva: '*It was through the help of my unknown mother that my well-known father was able to carry forward his work.*'

Unknown—and known! She tended his home, cooked his meals, tidied the children. Until recently, her name was unknown to many of us—but she made possible one of the most amazing ministries in this modern world.

Behind many a man in the public eye is a woman unknown. One has no call to be a 'feminist' to rejoice in this, or to forget it. Wordsworth wouldn't have been half the man—or half the poet—without his sister Dorothy behind him, home-making for him, and quickening his eye and spirit. And in fullest truth the same must be said of Tennyson. Without Emily, the gentle-hearted, how would he have got the literary criticism and encouragement he needed? Sunday by Sunday we sing the hymns of blind George Matheson—but let his biographer say it: 'The chief factor, undoubtedly, in his harmonious, successful, and marvellously fruitful life, was his sister.'

In our own day we have been moved by Sir Winston Churchill's tribute to 'Clemmie'. 'My marriage,' said he gratefully, 'was much the most fortunate and joyous event which happened to me in the whole of my life.' Field-Marshal Smuts, speaking at his own golden wedding, as charmingly phrased his tribute to the woman behind him: 'She is the steam in my kettle!' And one of our modern poets as clearly speaks for many a one:

> *I came back late and tired last night,*
> *   Into my little room.*
> *To the long stair, the firelight,*
> *   And comfortable gloom.*
> *And as I entered softly in*
> *I saw a woman there.*

74

Searching for a Saratoga

MY FRIEND, Dr Frank Boreham, as a shy young
man, once came on one whom he knew travelling
by train in Tasmania. She was in great distress—she
had lost her saratoga. With characteristic gallantry he
volunteered to search for it, and set off through the
train. His only difficulty—he admitted years later, with
a chuckle—was that he hadn't the vaguest idea what
he was looking for. A saratoga might be a pet animal,
or a piece of jewellery, or some kind of feminine under-
wear. He felt too shy to ask for details. Happily, after
some time, the girl herself recovered her lost property,
and to his relief, a saratoga turned out to be a travelling
trunk. The frantic, futile search for something he was
not sure about, always thereafter reminded him of
some people's search for happiness.

But happiness arises out of *being*, not out of *having*—
so in the strict sense, it can't be searched for. To dash
hither and thither is futile.

Jesus recognized the human need for happiness, and
straightway began His Sermon on the Mount at the
point of confusion. 'He opened His mouth and taught
them, saying: Blessed—*Happy*' (Mt 5$^{2-3}$). And He
repeated it. Aristotle had taught that the blessed life
was possible only to certain classes—it was not for
slaves, for the diseased, for the dying, or for the young.
The so-called 'happy' Greek set his heart on possessing
and worshiping things beautiful, art, and the lore of the
ages; the Roman, insolently proud and insatiable of
conquest, sought in another direction; the Jew centred

his search in dreams of national prosperity and greatness.

It was not surprising that upon the ears of the mixed company that listened to our Lord, His words should fall with paradoxical surprise. Happiness, He declared, is open to all; there is nothing exclusive about it; nor does it depend on things. To the unspoken question: 'How are the happy made happy?' He spoke plainly: '*How happy* are the humble-minded, for they already own the Kingdom of Heaven! *How happy* are those who know what sorrow means, for they will be given courage and comfort! *Happy* are those who claim nothing, for the whole earth will belong to them! *Happy* are those who are hungry and thirsty for goodness, for they will be fully satisfied! *Happy* are the kind-hearted, for they will have kindness shown to them! *Happy* are the pure in heart, for they shall see God! *Happy* are those who make peace, for they will be known as the sons of God! *Happy* are those who have suffered persecution for the cause of goodness, for the Kingdom of Heaven belongs to them! And what happiness will be yours when people blame you for My sake! Be glad then, yes, be tremendously glad—for your reward in Heaven is magnificent' (Mt 5^{1-12}, Phillips).

75

The Incarnation

'Do you think I would have danced it if I could have *said* it?' replied Pavlova, the great Russian dancer unforgettably, when asked what she meant by a certain dance.

And there are things like that—deeply spiritual things —when we say most by remaining silent. 'I want you to remember,' said Quintin Hogg, who poured out his life in Christian service for the poor boys of London, in a letter to one of them, 'that when God started to write a creed for us, He did it, *not in words that might change their meaning*, but He set before us a life, as though to teach us that whereas theology was a science which could be argued about, religion was a life.' And when due respect has been paid to the importance of theology, that is still true. That is the meaning of the Incarnation —in the fullness of time God sent forth His Son, made flesh to dwell among us. Now—

> *Mercy has a human heart,*
> *Pity a human face,*
> *And Love, the human form divine,*
> *And Peace, the human dress.*

God, to believing hearts, is no longer a glory in the heavens, He walks the ways of life known to men and women, He wrestles with our problems, He eats, drinks, sleeps, He faces Death—and rises triumphant above it. 'In Jesus Christ we have no mere doctrine about God, but the descent of God Himself.' This mightiest fact that we rejoice in, is much more than words—in the most down-to-earth sense, God in Christ shares our life, and gives us a share in His.

Words, for all their shining worth, have their limitations. It does not take us long to discover that; following our Lord, in this brash, bustling modern world we are 'called to be saints', but what does that mean? The phrase itself has an old-fashioned, other-worldly sound that doesn't in any way match the situation; it smacks of the thumb-screw and the cloister. Few in our modern day have realized the purpose of God in life more gloriously than Florence Allshorn. Returning from overseas, at the end of hazardous service, she set about the establishment of the training centre called St Julian's, and the interpretation of things Christian. How well she succeeded, how eloquent she was even in silence, is plain to many who rejoice in her life-story set down by Dr J. H. Oldham. In his Preface, he quotes the added witness of Miss Athene Seyler, the well-known actress. 'I only met Florence Allshorn a few times—over a supper table, at a bazaar, in church.' But she adds, 'Each time I had an unforgettable and almost incommunicable impression of something I had never encountered before, a feeling that she was living in two worlds simultaneously, mine and one she brought with her. . . . She was at once gay and yet profoundly serious around her gaiety. . . . She looked ready to share one's most trivial or sordid experience and one knew she would be untouched by it at the same time as bearing it. . . . I believe, of course, that I am trying to describe saintliness.'

How limited words are!

76

Cold Meat and Pickles

THE GUESTS have returned home. The fridge is full of bits—reminders of the succulent roast, and the pudding. All was temptingly hot when they gathered—now it's cold. Christmas, you say, is always like that—a tremendous season of preparation—then it's all over, and we're down to cold meat and pickles.

I like to think of the first Christmas. A great coming together it was; then as suddenly the inns had plenty of room. The crowds scattered, the officials gathered up the census-papers and sent them off, the litter left behind was collected, '*the shepherds*,' the Gospel says, '*returned*' (Lk 2²⁰). And if you look at it aright, that is full of significance. Once more they are tending their sheep.

But those first three words are not all—'*the shepherds returned*,' says the record, '*glorifying and praising God for all the things that they had heard and seen.*'

And that is still the secret for us. If our Christmas has been all that it should, nothing is ever the same again. Sheep-minding in the fields, counter-serving in the shop, dish-washing at the sink—nothing is the same. These day-to-day things take on a new dimension—God's little Child has been born into our life on earth. *And we return*, glorifying and praising God for all the things that we have seen and heard. We can't contrive ways of prolonging our Christmas celebration—we have to return. But what might easily seem like an anti-climax becomes its glory.

Luke loves to show us this pattern again and again

in his Gospel. Moving from the first Christmas, he tells of the Temptation of the young Master in the Wilderness. This is a critical experience for Him; and we are permitted through Luke a surprising amount of detail which must have come from Jesus Himself—for no one else was there. Then again with three strong words Luke says: 'And Jesus returned' (Lk 4¹⁴). Many things back in Galilee, after that absence of forty days, must have looked the same—and yet there was a difference. 'Jesus,' says Luke, 'returned in the power of the Spirit into Galilee.'

And Luke uses three words again, to tell us what happened after the Crucifixion. Amid the milling crowds, the body of the young Christ had been raised upon the Cross, stretched out between earth and heaven; now He had been laid in a sepulchre. Most, at this point, went their way—save the faithful women. 'And they returned,' says Luke, 'and prepared spices and ointments' (Lk 23⁵⁶).

Nor does the record end there; Luke rejoices to lay before us, as simply, the heart of the Ascension. The wonderful days of the sojourn of the Risen Lord now at an end, He takes His bodily leave of them. 'Then returned they,' says Luke (Acts 1¹²). '"Ye men of Galilee,"' ask two in white apparel, "why stand ye gazing up into heaven?" Then returned they unto Jerusalem.' And nothing was ever the same again. Such joy was in their hearts!

And God, in His mercy, I fully believe, intends that to be our experience!

77

At the Year's End

O F JOSHUA Scripture says: '*He left nothing undone*' (Josh 11¹⁵). How he achieved such a record is beyond me—and beyond most of us.

'This year's *omissions* have distressed me more than anything,' wrote Andrew Bonar. And we know only too well what he meant.

No heinous sins rise up to bother us—we have broken no law of the land, our names have been absent from the police-court news, we have not broken the Sabbath, been carried along by the modern gambling mania, failed to pay the grocer, or been ungenerous to missions. It is something else that worries us just now—not sins of commission, but sins of omission. Over-busyness, thoughtlessness, laziness, procrastination, these lie behind our unhappiness. 'To him that knoweth to do good, and doeth it not, to him it is sin,' says the New Testament, and the seriousness of this begins to dawn upon us. One by one we find ourselves taking up Marguerite Wilkinson's words:

> *I never cut my neighbour's throat;*
> *My neighbour's gold I never stole;*
> *I never spoiled his house and land,*
> *But God have mercy on my soul!*
> *For I am haunted night and day*
> *By all the deeds I have not done;*
> *O unattempted loveliness!*
> *O costly valour never won!*

More light has been ours than we have used—much more; more love than we have woven into life day by day—much more.

Our Lord's story of the pious Priest and Levite who passed by on the other side, attentive to the obligations of the Law, while the poor fellow, bludgeoned by the robbers, lay bleeding, makes uncomfortable reading. Guiltless of positive wrong-doing, they fell under His judgement simply by their failure to do what they might. No charge of exploiting the poor could be laid against Dives—for all we know, a respected citizen, he might have given liberally to the alms-box at the local synagogue; but in the final summing up all that we know for sure is that he failed to succour Lazarus who lay at his gate. And the burden of the Great Judgement scene, recorded in the Gospel, is the same (Mt 25). 'Inasmuch as *ye did it not*,' is the damning charge. 'I was an hungred ... thirsty ... I was a stranger ... naked ... sick ... and in prison.'

In modern times, our fellow-man lies beaten and robbed on many an international roadway on which the world hurries by; the wretched Lazarus lies un-heeded and un-helped on our very doorstep, because we are not looking for deeds of mercy so near home; our Lord goes hungry, thirsty, a stranger, because our day-to-day hospitality is not out-reaching, naked, because we have been slower than the moths to get round to the old clothes in our wardrobe, sick and in prison, because, decent citizens, we have had so many committees to attend, or superior, have lost patience with the vicious and the foolish who break the law.

So the year ends. May God have mercy on us;

our only comfort lies in the assurance that '*if we confess our sins, He is faithful and just to forgive us our sins*' (1 Jn 1⁹)—our sins of *commission*, and our sins of *omission*.

78

Not Forgotten

FEW MODERN historians, biographers, novelists, short-story writers can compare with the writer of Ecclesiastes in giving much in little. I can't recall anything to match the fifty-odd words of Ecclesiastes nine, verses fourteen and fifteen: 'There was a little city, and few men within it; and there came a great king against it, and besieged it, and built great bulwarks against it: Now there was found in it a poor wise man, and he by his wisdom delivered the city; *yet no man remembered that same poor man.*'

All the learned commentators are delightfully vague about this perfect thumb-nail sketch; is it history, they ask, folk-lore, or poetry? There is no way of being sure, at this date; but does it matter? As it stands, it provides, surely, the most perfect comment on many a human situation. In a moment of crisis, help from anyone is acceptable—but when the crisis is passed, it is all too easy to forget one's deliverer.

A refreshing exception has just come to my notice. From a friend who has served for years in the Solomon Islands, scene of some of the fiercest jungle warfare in the Second World War, I have received an attractive photograph of Ben Kevu, of Wana Wana Lagoon, and news of a recent very satisfying event.

Ben Kevu is the son of one Kere, a stalwart of the Methodist Church in earlier days, when its Gospel message was only being tested among a ferociously savage people, and to this day is a man loyal to his father's Church. He serves as a trusted Government clerk.

Away back in the old war days, when the grim fate of many of us hung in balance in the Solomons, Ben Kevu was one of a group of natives instrumental in bringing Lt. J. F. Kennedy and the crew of his P T boat to safety.

That was in 1943, and a lot of water has since passed through Blackett Strait where Kennedy's P T boat was hit by a Jap destroyer. Now Kennedy's name is known the world over as late President of the United States.

But what of the 'same poor man' who served him in that crisis? It is pleasant in this so-forgetful world, to be able to report that on his first trip out of the Solomons he was received at the White House by the President. He sat in his famous rocking-chair, and they reminisced; and out came the treasured O.H.M.S. envelope on which was written the fateful message from Reg Evans the coast-watcher which Kevu delivered.

Later, Kevu was able to meet all the crew members of Kennedy's P T boat—save one who, to the sorrow of all, had since died—and the third officer of the P T boat 109 the night the boat was rammed, took it upon himself to show their guest around.

The P T boat emblem tie-clasps that the President gave to Kevu will be treasured always—of that there is no doubt—but greater still will be the continuing warmth and satisfaction in the fact that, after all this time, one good man remembered.

79

Special Issue

I HAVEN'T KEPT it up, save for what I pop into the overseas mail-drawer of my desk. At ten, I was ready to exchange the orange, apple, or slab of cake in my lunch-bag for a new stamp—and frequently did. Adult stamp-collectors among my friends, I find, still take the matter as seriously, and I tear stamps off my envelopes for them.

They will rejoice that Dag Hammarskjold, Secretary-General of United Nations till his tragic death in the air-crash while going to cease-fire talks in the Congo, is remembered by special issues in several countries. Dutch Guiana was the first—with the 10 cents blue and the 20 cents purple carrying a fine portrait of the peace-maker, with the emblem of United Nations in the background.

This is a wholly fitting gesture, since Mr Hammarskjold was a stamp-collector himself; but chiefly that his work for our torn world may be remembered in the friendly correspondence and business undertakings of our common day. Dag Hammarskjold was more than a Swedish nobleman, a brilliant economist, an astute leader, he was a man of faith. In his speech at the opening of the Meditation Room in the U N building which I was privileged to visit in New York, he said: 'In this house with its dynamic modern architecture, there are very few things that give you the feeling of weight, solidity, and permanence. . . . In the seeming void of this room of Meditation we want to bring back the stillness which we have lost in our streets and in our conference rooms, and to bring it back in a setting in

...ould impinge upon the imagination
...simple truths, to the way in which the
...es gives life to the earth on which we
...ol to many of us of what the light of the
...man.' Of the great simple block of iron-
...centre, he said: 'We want this massive
...give the impression of something more than
.... We also had another idea which comes
...what, after all, we are trying to do here in this
...*we are trying to turn swords into ploughshares*, and
...ught we could bless by our thoughts the very
...ial out of which arms are made—iron-ore. It is
...terial which represents the very paradox of human
..., *the basic materials offered by God to us may be used*
...*her for construction or for destruction.'*

From the moment he assumed office, Hammarskjold
—miscalled by some, though not inappropriately
'Hammershield'—made it clear on which side he stood.
Introduced to the officers of the U N Assembly, he
moved down to the speakers' rostrum to say briefly:
'Ours is a work of reconciliation and realistic construction,' and to finish with the beautiful, relevant words
of a Swedish poet: '*The greatest prayer of man is not for
victory but for peace.*'

The shining clarity of his vision is shown to us by the
fact that on his last journey he carried but one book,
The Imitation of Christ—tucked inside it his Secretary-
General's oath of office.

It will be worthwhile if these special issues of stamps
serve to remind us of the alternatives in this age, and
of the deep, inner source of one man's positive devotion.
Jesus said: 'Blessed are the peace-*makers*'—and today
in our fateful situation, the emphasis must surely be on
that second word.

You flaunt no splendid plumage; Natu
In quiet tones of brown; indeed a small
And humble sparrow, yet at your final hour,
Is it not known, unheeded none shall fall?